1990

TOWARDS A LITERATURE OF KNOWLEDGE

TOWARDS A LITERATURE OF KNOWLEDGE

*

Jerome J. McGann

Did she put on his knowledge with his power
Before the indifferent beak would let her drop?

W. B. Yeats
'Leda and the Swan'

The University of Chicago Press

Chicago

Jerome J. McGann is Commonwealth Professor of English at the University of Virginia. Among his earlier books are *The Romantic Ideology: A Critical Investigation, A Critique of Modern Textual Criticism, The Beauty of Inflections: Literary Investigations in Historical Method and Theory*, and *Social Values and Poetic Acts: The Historical Judgment of Literary Work*.

The University of Chicago Press, Chicago 60637
Oxford University Press, Oxford OX2 6DP

Printed in Great Britain

98 97 96 95 94 93 92 91 90 89   5 4 3 2 1

Library of Congress Cataloging-in-Publication Data
McGann, Jerome J.
    Towards a literature of knowledge / Jerome J. McGann.
        p.   cm.
    Originally presented as series of four Clark lectures delivered at
Trinity College, Cambridge, February 1988 and delivered again at the
University of Chicago, May 1988.
    Includes index.
        ISBN 0–226–55839–8 (alk. paper)
        1. English poetry—19th century—History and criticism.   2. Truth
in literature.   3. Pound, Ezra, 1885–1972—Criticism and
interpretation.   I. Title.
PR585.T78M34 1989   88–25586
821'.009'384—dc19

This book is printed on acid-free paper.

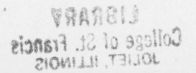

*This book is for Marjorie, and Marjorie,
masters of discourse who talked me into it*

Preface

Others abide our question. Thou art free.
  We ask and ask—Thou smilest and art still
Out-topping knowledge.

WE are fortunate that Arnold should have put his thought into a poetical form, into a sonnet as famous as any we have from the past two centuries. Reading 'Shakespeare' was to provide us with a touchstone for reading Shakespeare; and reading Shakespeare with that touchstone was to have supplied us with a touchstone for reading all poetical work. The style of 'Shakespeare' is crafted with great care so that it will, in its expository mode, find a way to rhyme with the abiding stillness Arnold wishes us to find in Shakespeare. How unlike this 'Shakespeare' is to the Shakespeare of 'On Sitting Down to Read *King Lear* Once Again', or—for that matter—to the Shakespeare of *King Lear* itself, which seems strangely imagined as inhabiting such an untroubled Arnoldian place.

Arnold's sonnet thus raises nothing but problems and questions, about 'Shakespeare' and about Shakespeare. Yet Arnold was wise beyond his thought to have cast his thought into this excellent verse, for in doing so he exposed the polemical character of what he was saying, and betrayed that secret of the imagination which he had been most anxious to preserve: that it makes statements, that it communicates, that its architectonics have designs upon us.

Eleven years ago, in 1977, I decided that it would be important to pursue this most closely guarded of the secrets of the imagination. I began with a series of essays in the field of literature and ideology, but this work quickly expanded to embrace problems in the theory of texts, canon-formation, periodicity, and a whole network of problems in the historiography of literary work, particularly during the past two centuries, and the sociology of literary institutions.

The secret of the imagination, that in its fictional forms it still deals in matters of truth and error, that it engages and promotes moral and political values, is very clear to me now. Indeed, it is clear to me that the secret was never a secret at all, that it has always left itself open to us, a plain text. None the less, I am also now aware that the secret has preserved its mystery; for, by a kind of Borgesian transformation, the secret has hidden itself in the labyrinth of its apparitions.

These lectures, therefore, complete that project which I initiated eleven years ago, when I began by thinking that I had discovered a great secret but came to see that what I had actually stumbled upon was a set of historical illusions. With that understanding the project changed into an effort to trace the recent history of those illusions, on one hand, and to raise a polemic against the ideas and institutions which seek to maintain those illusions on the other.

The focus of my argument in this book can be sharply defined: it is the tradition of aesthetic theory and interpretation which received its initial formulation in Kant, and which assumed its culminant statement in Gadamer's *Truth and Method* (1960). Part I section 3 of that monumental work summarizes the ground of this Kantian tradition, and I quote two related passages from it here to mark out my point of departure:

Where art rules, it is the laws of beauty that are in force and the frontiers of reality are transcended. It is the 'ideal kingdom', which is to be defended against all limitation.

What we call a work of art and experience aesthetically depends on a process of abstraction. By disregarding everything in which a work is rooted (its original context of life, and the religious or secular function which gave it its significance), it becomes visible as the 'pure work of art'.

If we follow Gadamer we shall think that he is here defining the 'being' of art, the nature of art *as such*. In fact, however, he is doing something else—he is setting out the grounds for a certain cultural project, for a particular way of dealing with those human productions we call 'art'. What Gadamer says here is, therefore, strictly true, but strictly in relative and historical terms. As we shall see, everything he postulates of art can be falsified. Beauty, transcendence, abstraction—none of these are necessities of art. Indeed, one purpose of this book is to show that even as the Kantian programme was developing and institutionalizing itself in the West between (say) 1790 and 1960, the practice of art was beating against those programmatic restrictions, and demonstrating—insisting—that it has, that it will always have, larger resources than may be dreamt of in philosophy.

My argument against this Kantian way of thinking about art and poetry will be developed by looking at four major writers whose

work was produced between approximately 1790 and 1960. Each
chapter here may be read as an independent discussion of the work
of Blake, Byron, D. G. Rossetti, and Ezra Pound. The presentation
as a whole, however, depends upon four interlocked ideas about the
way poetic discourse gets carried out—in the work of these four
writers particularly, but also in imaginative writing at large. Though
all four ideas might be illustrated from any of their work, I have
emphasized and associated one of these interlocking ideas with each
of the four writers.

So, out of Blake I try to show, principally, how poetry is a form of
action rather than a form of representation, and a form of action for
'Giving a body to Falshood that it may be cast off for ever' (*Jerusalem*,
12: 13); out of Byron that poetry's form of action is social, a communicative exchange; out of Rossetti that within the conventions of
Romanticism and post-Romanticism, the body of falsehood appears
initially as the author's body (or the body of what we would now call
'the author function'); and out of Pound that, as a socially dispersed
body of falsehoods, poetry's ultimate truth-function is to require that
the blind shall lead the blind. Poetry's acts of communication are
transmitted in those codes of ideology (i.e. 'false consciousness')
which are deployed by poetry's writers and readers.

In such contexts one may well speak of a 'social text', since we
have in mind the exchanges carried out between various writers and
readers. Furthermore, this 'social text' may be usefully studied at
three levels of its operation: what I have called (most recently in
'Theory of Texts', *London Review of Books*, 18 Feb. 1988, p. 21) the
level of the work, of the version, and of the text. The human exchanges
designated by the term 'social text' operate at each of the three
levels, and of course between the three levels as well. This means
that the particular projects and intentions of different individuals—
most crucially, those of the author and of the author's various
readers—become incorporated into many interactive networks. The
'social text' is the field—I do not think we can say, after Hegel, the
'organism'—where the various interactions play themselves out.

We prefer to speak here of a field rather than of an organism
because the latter, in this context, implies a whole which is (at any
rate) *capable of* entire self-consciousness. A field, by contrast, may or
may not be self-integrated, and while some fields are open to complete description, the Heisenberg principle ensures that even such
descriptions will be limited by their specular positions. Thus one

realizes the possibility of several—perhaps an indefinite number—
of 'complete' descriptions of a field, each of which is itself a part—or
rather, part of several parts—of the field itself.

Since the field of our interests, poetry, is a network of human
exchanges, however, it exhibits intentionalities at every point and
level. Thus intentional agents within the field—paradigmatically,
the authors and their readers—fall subject to various co-operative
designs and intentions. Communicative interaction is of course
common to all forms of discourse. It seems to be the special privilege
of poetical discourse, however, that its exchanges cannot be wholly
mastered by any of its intentional agents. Poems therefore exhaust,
expend, their agents, but are not themselves exhausted; this was
Bataille's great insight into the sociality of poetical work.

This book sets out to display the operations of that kind of social
text. In thus characterizing my own intentions, however, I have
deployed a trope of personification ('This book sets out . . . ') to
which I shall recur frequently in the course of the discussion. The
trope gestures toward the network of intentionalities which constitute
the field of the social text. More than that, however, the trope forces
one to confront the relative structure of intentional agency as it
operates in the field of the social text. I am the originary author of
this book just as Byron was the originary author of *Don Juan*. Nevertheless, this book and *Don Juan* come into—join, acquire, and develop
for themselves—meanings, designs, and purposes which supervene
the originary and authoritative ones.

Consequently, the trope that delivers intentionality to an 'author's'
work is a signal that we are working in a field of intentions, and that
none of those intentional structures or agents will ever be equal to
the entire set. By ceding authority to what must also be seen as the
creature or product of another authority, this tropic move turns
upside-down the traditional hierarchy of textual authority. The
move is not, however, to be taken as simply a transfer of authority
from one fixed point (the 'author') to another (the 'text'), and
neither is it to be understood as a complete undermining of all
authority. Rather, the move asks the reader to imagine the poetical
work as a kind of Mandelbrot set, where various local orders and
authorities emerge, shift the scale of their operations, and sometimes
pass out of view altogether. The entire *work* is never equal to itself—
it is always 'incommensurate'—even as it never ceases to operate by
design (or perhaps one should say by 'designs').

When Kristeva speaks of 'the writing subject' she gestures towards this kind of incommensurability. Foucault's 'author function' indicates a similar condition of textual non-identity. Kristeva's 'writing subject', however, seems to me a better term because it keeps us aware that we are dealing with human agency. If poetical discourse is to be seen as a field rather than an organism, we do better to treat it as a field of human subjects, and not a field of mathematical functions.

Because each of poetry's 'writing subjects' operates within the larger field, each works 'in subjection' to that field. Some of the writing subjects have greater authority than others, of course, but none is autonomous. For this reason it is essential, sometimes, to imagine the entire field, or poetical work, as the 'writing subject': the gesture obliges one to acknowledge that even the most masterful authorities—Lord Byron, Ezra Pound, the twentieth-century literary critic—are being written by the works to which they devote their authorities. Blake seems to have understood this subjection better than most. An artist like Rossetti, however, dramatizes precisely what is involved when a 'writing subject' becomes wholly dispersed into the writing field—when an 'author' is imagined, through the author's own work, to have become an 'author function'. I have organized the chapter on Rossetti as a biocritical narrative precisely to emphasize the purely nominal 'state' (to borrow a Blakean term) with which 'D. G. Rossetti' became absorbed.

This book originated as the series of four Clark Lectures which I delivered at Trinity College, Cambridge, in February 1988. I was asked to give the same lectures subsequently at the University of Chicago, as the William Ives Carpenter Visiting Professor of Humanities, in the following May. My thanks go to both of these institutions for the honour of their invitations, and in particular to Sir Andrew and Lady Huxley, Adrian Poole, Janel Mueller, and Jerry Mast. I benefited as well from the many conversations I had with the faculties and students during my time in Cambridge and Chicago.

Certain other people have, over the years, done much to help and encourage me in this work: Anne, Geoffrey, Christopher, and Jennifer McGann; Bruce Andrews, Charles Bernstein, Leo Braudy, Ron Bush, Marilyn Butler, Nick Dirks, Bob Essick, Cheryl Giuliano, Janet Kauffman, Jon Klancher, Jenijoy LaBelle, Cecil Lang, Marjorie

Levinson, Randall McLeod, Lee Patterson, Marjorie Perloff, Ron Silliman, Jeff Skoblow, John Sutherland, and my students at Johns Hopkins University and the University of Southern California. Finally, I am grateful to Jim Chandler, Beth Helsinger, Michael Murrin, Jay Schleusener, and Bob Von Hallberg for the gifts of their critical intelligence; they all intervened in the most fruitful ways during the final stages of this work.

J. J. M.

Contents

List of Illustrations

Introduction

> Now, in order to follow the true path, without being led astray by all
> the religious and philosophical gibberish, it is necessary to study the
> falsest of all false paths, philosophy.
>
> JOSEF DIETZGEN quoted by V. I. LENIN
> *Materialism and Empirio-Criticism*

> This demise of autonomy was . . . a task imposed upon art after it had
> become clear that the notion of autarky was untenable, both in
> philosophy and art. . . . Aesthetic experience must pass over into
> philosophy or else it will not be genuine.
>
> THEODOR ADORNO
> *Aesthetic Theory* (8. 12)

I

WHAT does it mean, a Literature of Knowledge? The phrase originates with De Quincey, who wanted to separate imaginative writing
(the Literature of Power) from scientific writing (the Literature of
Knowledge: political economy, natural philosophy, and so forth).
The distinction originates, however, in Wordsworth's discussion of
the social function of the poet in his 'Preface' to the *Lyrical Ballads*:

The knowledge both of the Poet and the Man of science is pleasure; but
the knowledge of the one cleaves to us as a necessary part of our existence,
our natural and unalienable inheritance; the other is a personal and
individual acquisition, slow to come to us, and by no habitual and direct
sympathy connecting us with our fellow beings. The Man of science seeks
truth as a remote and unknown benefactor; he cherishes and loves it in his
solitude: the Poet . . . rejoices in the presence of truth as our visible friend
and hourly companion. . . . Emphatically may it be said of the Poet, as
Shakespeare hath said of man, 'that he looks before and after.' . . . He is the
rock of defence for human nature. . . . In spite of difference of soil and
climate, of language and manners, of laws and customs . . . the Poet binds
together by passion and knowledge the vast empire of human society, as it is
spread over the whole earth, and over all time.[1]

Few passages in our cultural inheritance have been more influential
than this one. From our vantage, however, in the light of the sub-

---

[1] *Lyrical Ballads*, ed. R. L. Brett and A. R. Jones (London, revised 1965), 259.

sequent historical development of the 'two cultures', Wordsworth's eloquence dates itself. The Frankensteinian vision of the scientist as a figure of solitude seeking 'truth as a remote and unknown benefactor' is just as much a historically based ideological conception—a 'modern myth' of Prometheus, as Mary Shelley saw—as is its corresponding vision of poetry as the medium of 'human nature'. Wordsworth thinks that the scientist deals with what is particular and idiosyncratic whereas the poet's 'object is truth, not individual and local, but general, and operative'.[2] Yet today we should be at least as likely—indeed, I think more likely—to reverse Wordsworth's terms. Whereas the truth of science seems 'general, and operative', the truth of poetry would be 'individual and local'.

The difference arises because the 'human society' which is 'spread over the whole earth' has seemed for some time at least as alienated and fractured as it is bound 'together by passion and knowledge'— indeed, has seemed as bound by the chains of exploitation and various imperialisms as it is embraced in benevolence and sympathy. Wordsworth's vision might itself be best understood as an effort to defeat, at the imaginal level, those actual fragmentations and differentials 'of soil and climate, of language and manners, of laws and customs'. In this respect we could say of Wordsworth what Blake said of Los[s]—that he worked to keep the divine vision in a time of trouble.

Hence the truth-functions of poetry, in the line of thought epitomized by Wordsworth, have grown to seem increasingly displaced from actuality. Indeed this displacement, this resort to 'a world elsewhere', has been fashioned into a positive aesthetic. In this view poetry executes what Arnold would call 'a criticism of life'. The critique involves that negative or reactive movement by which it casts an anathema upon the social dysfunctions of actuality. Its corresponding positive dimension assumes one of two forms: it is seen either as the representation of the best that has been known and thought in the world, or as the image of a human power to transcend retrograde and adverse circumstances.

The so-called legitimation crisis in the human sciences has emerged in the gradual realization, during the past almost two hundred years, that this programme of truth, while it may be 'general', is not 'operative'. The programme has been carefully nurtured in the

---

[2] *Lyrical Ballads*, p. 257.

schools throughout this century, that is to say, throughout the period when it was showing itself increasingly irrelevant to either the practice of science or the practice of poetry and art. According to Jean-François Lyotard's acute report on education in *The Postmodern Condition*, the delegitimation of the humanities can be traced to their failure to meet the criterion of performativity.[3]

Lyotard's argument is essentially the same as that made by Peacock in 'The Four Ages of Poetry'—minus the mytho-historical trappings. Shelley's response to Peacock in many ways simply reformulates Wordsworth's earlier position; but whereas the dominant tropes in Wordsworth's argument are (as Shelley knew) nationalist and (as Coleridge lamented) associationist, Shelley's 'Defence' elaborates its materialist psychology within a much more broadly social and historical frame of reference. Consequently, Shelley's 'Defence' registers the crisis of an ideal of 'human nature' which is by no means 'spread over the whole earth, and over all time'. Shelley's sense of the emergencies of the imagination is linked to a double awareness: that social disintegration is institutionally promoted, and that poetry is itself an institutional (a legislative) force. Poetry, therefore, which is deeply involved in the crisis it reflects, may be seen either to maintain (like Wordsworth's 'Peter Bell') or to oppose (like Byron's *Cain*) the crisis it registers. This is why Shelley's 'Defence', unlike Wordsworth's 'Preface', can even imagine an actual, historical 'death' of imagination.

Wordsworth and Shelley are both great poets, but Shelley's theory of poetry—his knowledge and understanding of it—goes well beyond Wordsworth's. This is because Shelley is able to imagine imagination (or, more accurately, Romantic imagination) not as the solution to the problems it confronted, but rather as the latest and most acute instance and experience of those problems; and he is able to articulate this problem of imagination in his prose and his poetry alike. Shelley does this by making us realize, through his work, that poetic acts are not (as Arnold would have had it) 'free . . . still | Out-topping knowledge'. On the contrary, to the degree that they are at all involved with truth and knowledge, to that extent are they open to error, mistake, and the disconfirmations that follow from those conditions. Imagination and poetry can be wrong, can be evil, can even die.

This is possible to poetry and imagination because, as Blake saw

---

[3] *The Postmodern Condition: A Report on Knowledge*, trans. Geoff Bennington and Brian Massumi (Minneapolis, 1984).

so clearly, art is a set of actions carried out in the world. It is not disinterested and it is not occupied by 'virtual' space or 'virtual' realities. To imagine poetry in this way is to rob it of its truth-functions; it is to deliver it over to a truth and a freedom so absolute as to be both meaningless and inconsequential.

Blake's work is important, in this study, because it insists that poetry is not just a play or dance of language. The illuminated text is an index and a symbol of this translinguistic condition—a condition in which imagination comes to be figured as a deed of art, a performance in the world. The extreme unreality of Blake's materials—I mean his notorious personal mythology—simply reinforces the arbitrary, agented character of what Blake produces. Reality is what it is made to be and poetic truth is not conceptual; it is a process of knowing.

What Blake does not so clearly illustrate—the social and inter-active nature of art's performative function—is much more clearly seen by studying Byron. Byron's works are the field on which various transactions between an author and his audiences are carried out. Through him we understand how poetic truth emerges not merely as an action but as an interaction. In this situation the 'author function', as Foucault would later describe it, erupts into the consciousness of an artistic practice. The term 'Byronic' means precisely that the 'author' has become an artistic function, a hero (or a villain)—a character—in the works issued under the author's name. Such an 'author' comes into existence at the same moment as the *hypocrite lecteur*, who is what *Don Juan* calls the 'twin opposite' of the (equally hypocritical) 'author'.

That critical dynamic, made famous by Baudelaire's reading of Byron and Byronism, is most dramatically carried out in England by Dante Gabriel Rossetti. In his work, and pre-eminently in *The House of Life*, poetry chooses to interrogate itself with complete seriousness. Through a pitiless self-consciousness far outstripping even what Keats had done,[4] Rossetti admits—makes the admission and its significance his essential subject—that imagination and art are commodities. The demonstration of this truth is the project of his work, and the consequence is a series of inversions in our traditional understanding about what art and poetry involve. Most unnerving,

---

[4] For a discussion of Keats in this frame of reference see Marjorie Levinson's important and innovative study *Keats's Life of Allegory: The Origins of a Style* (Oxford, 1988).

perhaps, is the fall of 'beauty' as a foundational category of the artistic. This happens when it is shown that no transcendental distinction can be preserved between what is beautiful and what is horrible.

The insight is an important inheritance of twentieth-century culture: not merely that we have built our temples in excremental places, but—even more terribly—that 'there is no document of civilization which is not at the same time a document of barbarism'.[5] Of the Modernist poets who write in English, Pound illustrates a writing practice which fully pursues the truth of that understanding. After the radio broadcasts, after the DTC in Pisa, after St Elizabeth's, Pound, surveying his career, saw himself as the last American living out the tragedy of Europe.[6] If 'tragedy' is distinctly the wrong word here—'disaster' would have been far more appropriate—the insight none the less is deep, for it points towards the consequence suffered by a poetry and culture which had committed itself to power instead of knowledge, to tradition instead of truth.

II

From the point of view of science and philosophy, truth may be measured in one of two ways. Hilary Putnam, in his critique of the more traditional 'correspondence theory' of truth, calls them the 'externalist' and the 'internalist' perspectives. According to the former

There is exactly one true and complete description of 'the way the world is'. Truth involves some sort of correspondence relation between words or thought-signs and external things and sets of things.[7]

Such a view is opposed by 'a late arrival in the history of philosophy . . . the *internalist* perspective' (to which Putnam adheres):

'Truth', in an internalist view, is some sort of (idealized) rational acceptability—some sort of ideal coherence of our beliefs with each other and with our experiences *as those experiences are themeselves represented in our belief system*—and not correspondence with mind-independent or discourse-independent 'states of affairs'.[8]

---

[5] This is the famous aphorism of Walter Benjamin: see his *Illuminations*, ed. Hannah Arendt (New York, 1969), 256.
[6] See below, p. 127.
[7] *Reason, Truth and History* (Cambridge, 1981), 49.   [8] Ibid. 49–50.

In both cases 'truth' involves what Putnam calls (speaking only of an internalist view, however) *'ultimate goodness of fit'*.[9] The correspondence theory and the coherence theory of truth equally posit an ideal of part-to-whole orderliness.

Aesthetic theory since Kant has generally sought to preserve the truth-functions of poetry by appealing to Putnam's internalist perspective, with its criterion of coherence as the measure of truth. The development of that aesthetic, in fact, was no more than a second-order application of the Kantian programme, where the coherence theory of truth had been developed in a general way. The aesthetic ultimately came to dominate English studies through the work and the influence of Coleridge.

Blake's importance for the history of poetry during the past two hundred years lies exactly in the resistance he maintained to the view that truth in poetry is ultimate goodness of fit. His response to Wordsworth's version of that idea (as set forth in the *Recluse* fragment) is famous: 'You shall not bring me down to believe such fitting & fitted I know better & Please your Lordship'.[10] Blake's work might be described in many appropriate terms: intelligent, energetic, calculated, sensational. His critics sometimes charged it against him that his work lacked coherence, that it often seemed positively *in*coherent. But since Blake adhered to an inspirational (sometimes called 'prophetic') theory of poetry, the charge of incoherence is no more than an assertion that Blake's work does not meet an Apollonian truth-condition.

Blake's example sets the terms in which the present study has been cast. If we observe the practice of poetry through the antithesis he represents, we shall be inclined to one of two conclusions with respect to the issue of truth in poetry: either it is irrelevant with respect to the issue of truth, or poetry may have (must have?) truth-functions which are not encompassed by the coherence and correspondence theories of truth.

Since Plato's initiating arguments against the truth-functions of poetry, a whole series of 'defences' of poetry have been made. I shall not rehearse them here. Instead, I want to pick up the argument I began to develop in the opening section of *Social Values and Poetic Acts* (1988): that the truth-functions of poetry (and of imaginative work

---

[9] Hilary Putnam, *Reason, Truth and History*, p. 64.

[10] *The Complete Poetry and Prose of William Blake*, newly rev. edn. by David V. Erdman (Garden City, NY., 1982), 667.

in general) operate through the principle of incommensurability. Poetry is not irrational; rather, it is the one form of discourse we have which displays the fact that human reason—the mind—has more comprehensive means for dealing with truth than is suggested by the traditional arguments of philosophy.

Three matters are crucial here. The first is that the mind is not an abstract or abstracting power, though of course the power of abstraction is one of its functions. Human beings are not angels, and there is, consequently—as George Lakoff and Mark Johnson have recently been arguing with great effectiveness—a 'bodily basis of meaning, imagination, and reason'.[11] The physique of poetic discourse is the ultimate ground of its radical incommensurability, and that physique can take many forms within the three general areas in which discourse occurs: linguistic, bibliographical, transactive. In this book my examples and illustrations have been chosen to emphasize this quality of poetic discourse. The point can be summarized in the following aphorism: with respect to truth, experience always outruns conception.

In poetry, therefore, knowledge will appear as a form of activity rather than as a content, a possession, or an idea. To the degree that poetry is read thematically, to that extent it skirts what Blake called 'the wastes of Moral Law'. Because one of the chief activities of poetry is to read itself, to assume ideological positions with regard to its own activities, poetry can often be seen to undermine itself, to display those 'gaps' and 'ruptures' which current deconstructive analysis is so acute to realize. When we speak of the *critical* functions of poetry, what we usually have in mind is poetry's habit of moving against the grain of traditional ideas or attitudes. Because all poetry is invested in and by tradition in some way—because it is what Gadamer would call 'prejudiced', because it speaks out of certain frames of human interests—poetical works necessarily involve deconstructive critical functions as well. In such manœuvres poems seek—as certain scientists would say—to 'falsify' themselves.

Finally, to understand the thought-activity of poetic discourse means that we have to grasp the social character of human thinking. The truth-experience of poetry is always transactional—what Habermas, in a different context, spoke of as 'communicative action'.

[11] See George Lakoff, *Women, Fire, and Dangerous Things: What Categories Reveal About the Mind* (Chicago, 1987), and Mark Johnson, *The Body in the Mind: The Bodily Basis of Meaning, Imagination, and Reason* (Chicago, 1987).

The experience that outruns conception, in poetry as in all forms of discourse, is not 'authoritative', it is social. This means that a poem's incommensurability is replicated at the level of reception, and that what we call 'context' is the transactional dimension within which the bodily basis of meaning, imagination, and reason plays itself out.

In this frame of reference we shall find that poetry possesses ideological investments, and that within its fictional space it still delivers—sometimes forthrightly, sometimes in ciphered texts— opinions, ideas, even *propositions*. Unlike other kinds of discourse, however, poetry's expositions and arguments are always set in their entire context of controversy. That interactive field opens the text to many kinds of readings—co-operative and descriptive readings, analytical and dissenting readings, readings that move upon the text at strange diagonals, or that leap away from the text altogether in imaginative flights of their own. Nor is the text ever 'free' of those engagements and disengagements: it abides their questions, including their differences and indifferences; for the readings are themselves meshed in their own various commitments, and the texts—for better and for worse—will have something to say in return. Poems may be at the mercy of their readers, but readers find themselves equally at the hazard of the texts.

'The truth, the whole truth, and nothing but the truth.' This is the apophthegm under which poetry is compelled to operate. Those who decide to engage seriously in its discourse will therefore proceed at their own risk: *caveat scriptor, caveat lector*.

CHAPTER I

William Blake Illuminates the Truth

Poetry is like a swoon
with this exception:
it brings you to your senses.

CHARLES BERNSTEIN
'The Klupzy Girl'

WHAT is the truth of imagination? I shall put this question to four
different poets, each of whom has something different to say on the
subject. All four—Blake, Byron, Dante Gabriel Rossetti, and Pound—
have much in common, though they could hardly be characterized
as a 'line' or poetic tradition; and Rossetti in particular stands apart
from the other three in some obvious ways. But how each one dealt
with the question of imagination and truth throws into sharp relief
some of our central conceptions, and misconceptions, about poetry
and criticism.

I begin with Blake because he is, I think, an originary figure in the
modern revaluation of what we call, after Blake himself, 'imagination'.[1] The point of departure will not be, however, any of those well-
known texts where Blake deals conceptually with either 'truth' or
'the imagination'. I start rather from the opening text-page (plate 3)
of Blake's consummate work *Jerusalem*, which offers an address 'To
the Public'.[2]

The plate contains a sort of Preface to the poem, a set of remarks,
some in verse and some in prose, which were to help 'explain' what
the subsequent work imagines itself to be doing. *Jerusalem* is a public

[1] But see the discussion of Wordsworth in the Introduction.

[2] All my texts for the illuminated books are taken from the Trianon Press
facsimiles. The non-illuminated texts are from *The Complete Poetry and Prose of William
Blake*, newly rev. edn. by David V. Erdman (Garden City, N.Y., 1982). Engraved
texts are identified in the text by plate- and line-number; other texts by citation to the
Erdman edition (E) by page-number. I wish to add here that this chapter was
completed before I could take the full benefit of Donald Ault's important study of
Blake, *Narrative Unbound: Revisioning William Blake's The Four Zoas* (Barrytown, NY,
1987). Much of Ault's work overlaps with my own; I have been reading preliminary
studies from his book over the past ten years, so that his work has been a constant and
crucial presence to my own.

performance from 'the mouth of a true Orator', Blake says; its audience is 'the Human Race', and most immediately the nation of Great Britain; it is a work of deliberate art ('Every word and every letter is studied'), but equally a piece of unpremeditated verse— inspired work, 'dictated' to its 'printer' William Blake; and—though Blake does not indicate this explicitly—it comes from the same 'God' who years before had dictated *The Marriage of Heaven and Hell*, a dweller in flaming fire whose voice is not easily distinguished from Blake's own mind and conscience. Finally, the work is executed through what Blake calls 'my types', an obvious paronomasia that draws an equation between the poem's spiritual designs and its material orders.

Works of imagination traffic in paradoxes—those opposite and discordant qualities which we may believe poems set out to balance and reconcile. Plate 3 of *Jerusalem*, however, offers at least one paradox which the imagination will not comfortably seize as beauty. Physicalized on the plate itself, this paradox is eventual, not conceptual. Blake's text assures his reader that what he prints in the monumental and prophetic work he is calling *Jerusalem* will not be done in 'vain', but this opening page of *Jerusalem* has much of its own message gouged from the plate. The consequence is not simply a set of awkward transitions and distracting blank spaces, it is positive incoherence. These have been aptly called Blake's 'self-destructive deletions' because they 'withdraw . . . the affectionate terms addressed to the once-dear Reader, [and] effac[e without] . . . quite thoroughly effacing the poet's confessions of faith and enthusiasm'.[3]

We must remember that the condition of plate 3 is not 'momentary' or transitional in the sense that Blake simply neglected to make the necessary further alterations which would have restored coherence to his work. Blake had at least ten years, 1818–28, when he might have changed plate 3, given it some kind of verbal coherence. But he preserved a scarred discourse as the opening of this text, so that plate 3 must be regarded as what textual scholars sometimes call 'the author's final intentions'. Every surviving copy of *Jerusalem* exhibits a plate 3 mutilated in just this way, including the copies he sold during those last ten years, including even the magnificent

[3] David V. Erdman, 'Suppressed and Altered Passages in Blake's *Jerusalem*', *Studies in Bibliography*, (1964), 1–54; and 'Blake's *Jerusalem*: Plate 3 Fully Restored', ibid. (1965), 281–2.

SHEEP   GOATS

To the Public

After my three years slumber on the banks of the Ocean, I again
display my Giant Forms to the Public: My former Giants & Fairies
having reciev'd the highest reward possible: the   and
of those with whom to be connected, is to be   . I cannot doubt
that this more consolidated & extended Work, will be as kindly
reciev'd ~~~~~~~~~~~~~ The Enthusiasm of the following Poem, the
Author hopes

                                                                    I also
hope the Reader will be with me, wholly One in Jesus our Lord, who
is the God   and Lord   to whom the Ancients lookd
and saw his day afar off, with trembling & amazement.
    The Spirit of Jesus is continual forgiveness of Sin: he who waits
to be righteous before he enters into the Saviours kingdom, the Divine
Body: will never enter there. I am perhaps the most sinful of men!
I pretend not to holiness! yet I pretend to love, to see, to converse with
daily, as man with man: & the more to have an interest in the Friend
of Sinners. Therefore [dear] Reader,   what you do not approve, &
    me for this energetic exertion of my talent.

        Reader!   of books!   of heaven,
        And of that God from whom
        Who in mysterious Sinais awful cave.
        To Man the wondrous art of writing gave,
        Again he speaks in thunder and in fire!
        Thunder of Thought, & flames of fierce desire:
        Even from the depths of Hell his voice I hear,
        Within the unfathomd caverns of my Ear.
        Therefore I print; nor vain my types shall be:
        Heaven, Earth & Hell, henceforth shall live in harmony

            Of the Measure, in which
            the following Poem is written

We who dwell on Earth can do nothing of ourselves, every thing
is conducted by Spirits, no less than Digestion or Sleep.

    When this Verse was first dictated to me I consider'd
a Monotonous Cadence like that used by Milton & Shak-
speare & all writers of English Blank Verse, derived
from the modern bondage of Rhyming; to be a necessary
and indispensable part of Verse. But I soon found that
in the mouth of a true Orator such monotony was not
only awkward, but as much a bondage as rhyme itself.
I therefore have produced a variety in every line, both
of cadences & number of syllables. Every word and
every letter is studied and put into its fit place: the
terrific numbers are reserved for the terrific parts—
the mild & gentle, for the mild & gentle parts, and
the prosaic, for inferior parts: all are necessary to
each other. Poetry Fetter'd, Fetters the Human Race!
Nations are Destroy'd, or Flourish, in proportion as Their
Poetry Painting and Music, are Destroy'd or Flourish! The
Primeval State of Man, was Wisdom, Art, and Science.

full-coloured copy E which Blake prepared so carefully towards the end.[4]

This is truly an extraordinary situation, and yet the interpreters of Blake's *Jerusalem* pay very little attention to it when they discuss the work.[5] We should have to *imagine* comparable examples in the history of literature and poetry before our period, for nothing equivalent exists in fact. What Blake has done in *Jerusalem* is what Milton might have done had he excised certain phrases and lines from the opening twenty-six verses of *Paradise Lost*: had he excised, that is, passages carrying real weight and significance for the proem, and had he then printed and broadcast the poem with the lacunae left visible.

Blake did not *begin* his last epic work as a broken text, he *finished* it that way. The difference is crucial. Such a text calls attention to itself as gestural, performative. However it is to have its 'meaning' 'interpreted', the ruptured text of plate 3 is at least making the following representations: that the words and figures on such a page are abitrary, and that they were put there by design (in at least two senses).

The printed book is one of the most illusionistic of human works, imputing as it does an aura of permanence to the discourses we manipulate. Anyone who has taught knows the kind of authority which the book-form in itself lends to the words it contains. That illusionary authority only increased in the age of mechanical reproduction, as Benjamin has so brilliantly shown.[6] Thus both Tennyson and D. G. Rossetti confessed that they could hardly believe in the reality of their poems until they saw them put into print.

[4] All discussions here of the copies of Blake's books draw heavily on the monumental work by Gerald E. Bentley, Jr., *Blake Books* (Oxford, 1977).

[5] See above, n. 3. The only other comments that are more than just passing references are in the excellent review of David Erdman's revised edition of *The Complete Poetry and Prose of William Blake* by the Santa Cruz Blake Study Group (*Blake: An Illustrated Quarterly*, 18 [1984], 4–30); and in James Ferguson, 'Prefaces to *Jerusalem*', in Michael Phillips (ed.), *Interpreting Blake* (Cambridge, 1978), 164–95. Unlike the Santa Cruz Blake Study Group, Ferguson does not really grasp the problematic character of the plate (see e.g. his discussion at pp. 166–7): 'The deletions which Blake made from this plate reveal a growing sense of determination, and perhaps also of isolation, similar to that experienced by Ezekiel at the beginning of his prophetic work. . . . So, Blake deletes any apologies for his poem, clearly demonstrating a new awareness of prophetic calling, and exhibiting a much tougher attitude toward the reader' (167). This 'reading' has not come to grips with the *textual* ground of the 'hermeneutical' problem.

[6] See Walter Benjamin, 'The Work of Art in the Age of Mechanical Reproduction', in *Illuminations*, ed. Hannah Arendt (New York, 1969), 217–52.

In this respect, however, the book-form tends to depersonalize communication—to turn the transactions of language and other visible semes into what we now call 'discourse'. Poems are grasped as forms, as structures. Because plate 3 of *Jerusalem* does not permit one to read the text in those terms, however, it stands as an epitome of Blake's entire life's work. Simply considered from the perspective of external form, few of his poems have integral or unitary 'texts': there are dozens of orders for the *Songs*, for example, three for *The Marriage of Heaven and Hell*, several for each of the major epics, and *The [First] Book of Urizen* is notoriously protean. A major theme in his works, as we have known for some time, is their own productive processes—a topic which is raised not merely at the conceptual level, but *visibly* and concretely, as an issue of Blake's daily (changing) practice as writer, printer, engraver, and painter.

These matters point toward Blake's peculiar aesthetic activism. 'Beauty' is for him a function of 'energy', 'enthusiasm', and the display of ornamental and decorative invention. Reynolds's concern with order and 'Central Form' is to Blake a sign of imaginative poverty, and a failure to understand that art is founded on a profusion, an excess, of carefully articulated and minutely distinguished details. Nor is this a view he held only in the 1790s. Late in his career, around 1821, he was still making public declarations like those in the engraved manifesto *On Homer's Poetry*: 'Unity & Morality are secondary considerations & belong to Philosophy & not to Poetry'. The work of art is the display of the artist's imaginative energy. It is fundamentally an action, and to the degree that the 'completed' work reveals it *as* an action, the work is successful. Such an activity then tries to call out in the reader/viewer/audience a reciprocating response.

What art displays and generates in this communicative exchange is what Blake calls 'Intellect'. The term is not to be understood abstractly, as we can see when Blake speaks of the 'Arrows of Intellect' (*J* 98: 7), and of 'wars . . . With intellectual spears' (*J* 38: 14–15). 'Thought is Act' (E 612), he says in his critical annotations of Bacon, and art is more an execution (rather than a structure) of intellectual activities. In this respect his attacks upon 'Reason' are not only a promotion of 'Minute Particulars' over abstract ideas. He is arguing that poetry must be grasped as a type of communicative action.

This argument—and his work is, from the outset, very much a

series of arguments—disputes the truth claims of what used to be called rational and natural philosophy (or what we now call philosophy and science). Both are attacked under the respective names of 'Reasoning' (or sometimes 'Deduction') and 'Demonstration'. His case against them is not, of course, put into a 'philosophic' form; it is cast imaginatively, that is, as a sequence of interconnected images which carry their authority and 'truth' on their faces.

Blake's critiques of philosophy and of science, though related, are not identical. Both critiques begin from a pair of characteristic Blakean assumptions. First, he insists that 'Intellect' is not a *tabula rasa* but an activity working through a set of 'Innate Ideas'. These he commonly calls 'Eternal Forms', and whereas some are the equivalent of what Kant would call 'categories'—for example, the categories of Space and Time—many recall Plato's 'forms' and 'universals'. For Blake, no one invents, no one has ever invented, the 'forms' named horse, tree, city, god, or even man. These pre-exist the times of their many, and infinitely various, appearances. They are fundamental forms of truth, coextensive with the human world. Secondly, Blake assumes that the 'knowledge' which individuals gain in time and history is not acquired 'naturally'. 'Understanding or Thought is not natural to Man it is acquired by means of Suffering & Distress i.e Experience. Will, Desire, Love, Rage, Envy, & all other Affections are Natural. But Undertanding is Acquired' (E 591). From these two grounds Blake launches his attack upon those respective types of 'consecutive reasoning' embodied in philosophy and science.

'He who does not Know Truth at Sight is unworthy of Her Notice' (E 648) Blake declares. This is a remarkable formulation for several reasons. In the first place, the personification establishes 'Truth' as a transactional function—not a goal to be achieved through effort or pursuit, but a 'being' with whom one enters an intimate, a reciprocal, ultimately an erotic relationship. The Platonic tradition of Blake's thought is especially clear in this text. Furthermore, and as we shall see more clearly later, the parties to this erotic transaction are here imagined to be equally active: 'Truth' exists *both* in the eye of the beholder *and* as an independent, objective condition or 'being'. This carries an important consequence we shall have to explore in some depth: that the knower and the known, the subject and the object, shift their identities with respect to each other. That dialectical relativity exposes the imaginative and critical resources which are a special feature of poetical and artistic (as opposed to philosophical and scientific) discourse.

Of course, Blake personifies 'Truth' in this way partly because of his views on Innate Ideas, and partly because he wants to disengage 'truth' from 'morality'. For Blake, what is right and wrong, or good and evil, are matters of what we might call 'ideology' (in the classical Marxist sense of 'false consciousness'); Blake uses the traditional term 'Opinion'. But Blake's 'truth' and 'Intellect' have nothing whatever to do with ideology or opinion. The 'truth' to Blake is everything that is possible to belief and imagination (*Marriage* 8).

Consequently, the difference between the knowledges promoted by poetry on one hand, and by rational philosophy on the other, lies in this: whereas rational philosophy distinguishes good from evil and right from wrong, poetry distinguishes 'truth' from 'error'. In this respect poetry exposes the ideological content of philosophy. Blake's marginalia in Boyd's translation of Dante's *Inferno* declare the difference he sees between the poet (Dante) and the philosopher (Boyd). 'Poetry is to excuse Vice & shew its reason & necessary purgation' (E 623). That is what Dante does. But because Boyd writes about poetry as something which inculcates 'the difference between right and wrong', because he goes to poetry for ideas and themes, he shows that he is nothing but an ideologue. Therefore Blake dismisses him by saying simply: 'The grandest Poetry is Immoral. . . . Cunning & Morality are not Poetry but Philosophy'.

When Blake turns to argue poetry's credentials against natural philosophy, he takes a different line. For natural philosophy, unlike rational philosophy, represents itself as unconcerned with moral issues. 'Good' and 'evil' seem as unimportant to the scientist as they do to the poet. Blake's admiration for Paine and other enlightenment figures originates in his approval of their critical purposes, on the one hand—their exposure of 'priestly' hypocrisy—and, on the other, in his sympathy with their pursuit of knowledge through experience.

As time passed, however, and especially after the turn of the century, Blake's sympathies shifted dramatically. This turn is seen most clearly in the approving ways he comes to talk about 'Superstition', for example, or in his elevation of that prototypical enemy of enlightenment, the monk. Blake turns to attack enlightenment for its lack of faith, which is to say for its failure to see that knowledge is grounded in Innate Ideas. A correlative argument attacks enlightenment for its attachment to 'Nature', for its 'cunning' recapitulation of the old 'priestly' codes of morality under new forms of 'worldly' wisdom. But people must not be taught to accommodate themselves to the 'chaos' that is this world, which to Blake is a delusion of 'the mortal and perishing nature' (E 541) and a place of pain and suffering. What must be taught are not the ways of the world but the ways of Eternity—the latter being, in fact, ways of moving through this world, beyond it even as one appears to live under its dominion.

The ideological form which this scheme took is well known: it is antinomian Christianity. In themselves—apart from his imaginative works—Blake's ideas carry a certain historical importance, and the way his ideas change over time is also interesting to track. But we are not drawn to the ideas as such; rather, it is the poetry, and especially the illuminated work, which reveals Blake's intellectual power and significance.

This distinction is extremely important to grasp. We begin to see it clearly when we study his non-imaginative texts like the marginalia, the *Descriptive Catalogue*, and the 'Vision of the Last Judgment'. Blake works always under what he calls 'a firm persuasion', but when he engages intellectual debate in these kinds of texts, he typically resorts to bullying, name-calling, and mere assertion. His annotations are littered with explosives like 'Fool', 'Liar', 'Sly Dog', 'Villainy', and so forth. In this respect, Blake's firmly persuaded manner is not at all unlike what we shall later encounter in the texts of Ezra Pound, and especially Pound's prose texts and radio speeches. Blake's annotations are colourful and often important for illuminating parts of his imaginative works. None the less, they hardly bear comparison with, for instance, Coleridge's annotations, which move with such probing curiosity through their exploratory engagements and self-engagements. Blake learns little from his reading except the confirmation of his own 'innate ideas'. Unlike the intellectual prose of Coleridge, or Shelley, or even Wordsworth, Blake's does not command our interest or study.

Paradoxically, this stubborn insularity of mind produced, in his imaginative works, a truly epochal understanding and representation of the truth-functions of poetical discourse. Indeed, these works are not only properly to be called 'philosophical', they embody a philosophy of imagination, or an imagination of mind, which stood in the sharpest critical relation to the philosophical (and imaginative) spirit of the age.

II

Blake's antithesis comes more clearly into focus when we pose the following question: is poetical discourse a form of action or a dance of forms? When Arnold said that Pope and Dryden were masters of English prose, and when Coleridge earlier developed the English variant of Kant's theory of poetry, they were giving their allegiance to the view that poems are formal structures.[7] Cassirer's *Philosophy of Symbolic Forms* (1923–31) and Gadamer's *Truth and Method* (1960) are the completed statements of this position, which came to dominate language theory, hermeneutics, and poetics during the twentieth century.

But the decisive battles over the issue were fought between 1789 and 1824. If one observes that contest from within the period when it took place, one would have to judge that the outcome was inconclusive. Among the English Romantic poets, Blake, Shelley, and Byron were the key champions of the rhetorical position, whereas Wordsworth, Coleridge, and Keats laid the foundations of the theory of symbolic forms. Only later, in the actual history of English poetry and hermeneutics, did it become very clear that the symbolic position had won the day. Byron may have been the most celebrated writer of his period—to be ranked with Goethe alone—but in the one hundred years after his death we observe his gradual displacement as the pre-eminent figure of his age in England. His position had been usurped by Wordsworth and Coleridge.

Furthermore, those same one hundred years laid the foundation for 'readings' of Blake and Shelley which would make them citizens within this new ordering of the poetic tradition. Since all poems are at one level always a dance of forms, this interpretation of their work was always available. Moreover, the recondite surface of both Blake and Shelley made them especially susceptible to this kind of reading, which began with the Pre-Raphaelites and was canonized in the important work of W. B. Yeats.

That brief history is important to remember—along with its continuations in the work of commentators like Frye, Abrams, and Bloom—because we are now beginning to see how strange a history

[7] See Frank Lentricchia's *After the New Criticism* (Chicago, 1980), where Kant's crucial function in the process of aestheticizing poetic discourse is set forth (see esp. p. 41); and see also Karen Shabetai, 'Blake's Antifoundationalist Poetics', *Studies in English Literature*, 27 (1987), 555–70.

it is. Byron was of course never really assimilated to such a history, so that in the twentieth century he became a marginal presence in the institutional re-presentations of symbolistic histories of imagination. For him, poetry was a deed of language—the dance of forms as a mode of communicative action. But whereas we can see that Byron was one of the last important exemplars of that (once dominant) poetic position, we are only beginning to grasp the full dimensions of Blake's poetic programs for social intervention.

Not that we are unaware of Blake as the 'prophet against empire'. David Erdman is merely the most distinguished name among many who have elucidated Blake's political and social engagements. Indeed, so obvious is that aspect of Blake's work that it constitutes one of the three principal 'lines' of Blake criticism—the other two being the study of his symbolistic/allegorical methods, and of his work as an artist and engraver. The history of Blake studies has been a history of experimental alliances between these three distinct interpretative schedules, and of the uncertain results which have emerged. During the past ten years, for example, Blake's visual and verbal media have often been married in order to deepen the hermeneusis of his symbolic discourse.

Blake as visionary poet, Blake as the prophet against empire, Blake as painter and engraver. That is a heteronomous image, as if drawings on different planes were superimposed at slightly skewed angles. By contrast, the contradictions in figures like Coleridge and Wordsworth, or even Keats, hardly seem contradictions at all. We typically move through their work by manipulating sets of polarities within synthesizing hermeneutic programmes. This is difficult to do with Blake for two reasons.

In the first place, the tension between his visionary imaginings and his socio-political programme is expressed in the most extreme, not to say bizarre, forms. All early readers who had a chance to see a work like (for example) *Jerusalem*—from Southey and Crabb Robinson to Rossetti and Swinburne—were struck not merely by its obscurity, but by its clarity: that is to say, the clarity of its wild anomalies. 'A perfectly mad poem' Robinson called it, not without reason (as Blake himself might have ironically observed).[8] The index of its madness appears in Blake's habit of making what seemed inappro-

<hr/>

[8] See Gerald E. Bentley, Jr., *Blake Records* (Oxford, 1969), 229. For a useful survey of Blake's reputation see Deborah Dorfman, *Blake in the Nineteenth Century* (New Haven, 1969).

priate correlations—for example, locating people and places from ancient Israel, early Britain, and contemporary Europe in the same referential field, and then superimposing on those nominations complex networks of symbolic forms which were themselves non-uniform and unstable.

These materials are not easily synthesized, but equally problematic is the physique and radical immediacy of Blake's work. By casting his poetic imaginations in graphic forms—crucially, by engraving and scripting and even painting his words, and fusing them with elaborate decorative elements at every level—Blake turned out a 'poetry' which is as close to iconic and even ideogrammatic as it is possible to achieve in an alphabetic mode. Reading Blake is a physically demanding task, as everyone knows who has confronted what have been aptly called those 'walls of words' on the plates, especially in *Milton* and *Jerusalem*.[9] Of course, these difficulties can be ameliorated for the reader, as they commonly are when his work is read in those Lamb-like 'Tales from Blake' invented by our many subsequent typographical texts.

So far as the history of poetry is concerned, Blake's work is epochal. We should do better, when launching ourselves into the poetry of the nineteenth and twentieth centuries, to take *Songs of Innocence and of Experience* and *The Marriage of Heaven and Hell* as our points of departure than, for example, *Lyrical Ballads*. I say this because Blake's two revolutionary works throw into the sharpest relief (in several senses) the crisis which poetry was just then beginning to undergo, both institutionally and ideologically. Before this period, the relation of literature to society was relatively unproblematic at the level of social and political structures. These structures were somewhat loosened with the development of a 'public sphere' of discourse in the eighteenth century. Indeed, the work of certain writers in that period distinctly forecasts the tensions that would soon dominate literary work. These are prototypically fiction-writers, like Defoe and Smollett, whose constant literary struggles highlight not merely the growing connection between literature and commerce, but between literature and the market-place (that is, the world where people come to buy, or not to buy). But the same tensions are just as clearly forecast in poets like Chatterton and Macpherson, whose work represents an early attempt to reinvent invention—

---

[9] See Vincent De Luca, 'A Wall of Words: The Sublime as Text', in Nelson Hilton and Thomas A. Vogler (eds.), *Unnam'd Forms* (Berkeley, 1986), 218–41.

literally, to construct a new exponent for imaginative work. In Rowley and Ossian we recognize a poetry whose commitments to autonomy and integration appear all the more extreme because the commitments are felt to be under threat. The poems of Ossian are completely integrated into Ossian's world; and they are integrated because that world has been imagined and then engulfed within the poetic invention. The integration of Rowley and Ossian is, therefore, a critical statement about the disintegration experienced and observed by Chatterton and Macpherson in their sublunary world. It is poetry about a poetry which is having difficulty defining a sense of its social and institutional place.

Blake's work is emphatically of the same sort, only in Blake the problems are far more brilliantly defined and clarified. The institutional reasons for this advance are centred on Blake's position as an engraver. Working in that medium entailed costs in time and materials which writers did not have to sustain. Furthermore, as an artist Blake operated in a system where patronage, commissions, and institutional authority put far greater restrictions on individual freedom than those experienced by writers at this time. And among artists, engravers were the least powerful and least favoured group, without even the right to belong to the newly founded Royal Society.

Had Blake chosen a less elevated and more popular mode of discourse—had he been a Gillray or a Rowlandson—his career would have been made less complicated, if not less easy. But because, like the other Romantics, Blake had aspirations 'which pointed to the stars',[10] his institutional place only served to intensify the oppositional salient of a man brought up through radical and dissenting traditions and come to maturity in the revolutionary context of the late eighteenth century. Thus Blake occupied an extreme and marginalized position, as we know. Because this extremity was so peculiarly and complexly structured, however, it was a position from which compromises were not easily made, and even less easily maintained. Forms and avenues of accommodation were open, for example, to Fuseli, or the Lake Poets, or even Byron, but they were not there for Blake.

The balance and reconciliation of opposite and discordant qualities form no part, therefore, of Blake's programme and works. As we shall see, he does everything he can to destabilize his texts and

---

[10] The phrase is from *The Prelude* (1850), VI. 587.

prevent readers from turning them into what he derisively called 'forms of worship'. His works are (he says) 'poetic tales', but they avoid the narrative orderings that we expect to find in stories, and that we do find even in the most twisted of conventional tales (for example, in Blake's own day such Gothic fictions as *Melmoth the Wanderer*). His works are also (he says) 'Demonstrations', but they do not follow any ordinary discursive continuities, or what he called elsewhere 'worldly demonstrations'. Most of them do not even arrive at a point we could properly call a 'conclusion': his works end, but they do not generate the 'sense of an ending'. He denounced at length Sir Joshua Reynolds's rational 'principles' of art, but had he taken the trouble to annotate Kant's third treatise, or any of those texts in which Coleridge laid down his new 'organic' principles of poetry and imagination, he would have registered an equal and correspondent disgust. For Blake's art is ornamental and rhetorical, not organic and formal.

The issues at stake were both clear and momentous in his mind. Social conditions at all periods, and not least during the turbulent period of his own work, seemed to him a function of whether 'true art' was 'practised' or 'depressed'. The war with France was seized as proof that 'knaves' were dominating the arts of England. His two greatest works, *Milton* and *Jerusalem*, strove to break that domination, to make a revelation of 'true art' and the human orders it brought with it. Produced in a dark time—between 1803, when England and France re-engaged their war, and 1818, when the restoration of the European thrones had been finally accomplished—these works were meant to save the divine vision in a time of trouble: to provide exempla of how that salvation was always being carried out.

To call this, as Blake did in *Jerusalem*, his 'great task' is therefore hardly an overstatement. What kind of work could possibly be adequate to such a task, or what kind of workman? and what bearing does plate 3 of *Jerusalem* have upon those problems?

III

The answer to these questions is bound up with Blake's struggle with philosophy in its double guise. '[T]he Holy Reasoning Power' (*J* 10: 15) produces, through negative acts of 'distorted & reversed Reflexion' (*J* 17: 42), 'Doubt & Experiment' (*J* 54: 18), 'A Polypus of Roots of Reasoning Doubt Despair & Death' (*J* 69: 3). It equally

generates a desire for systematic and ordered truth, a solid, un-
fluctuating righteousness for which Blake gives those many wonderful
names corresponding to its many horrible forms (Urizen, 'the Rock
of Ages', the 'wastes of moral law', and so forth). As doubt and
righteousness are the 'truths' of philosophy, the truth of poetry, for
Blake, will be the set of their inversions.

His most famous statement of his programme is contained in the
following pair of lines from *Jerusalem*: 'I must Create a System, or be
enslav'd by another Mans | I will not Reason & Compare: my busi-
ness is to Create' (*J* 10: 20–1). The passage is worth pondering. We
understand (perhaps) the difference between 'reasoning' and
'creating', but why choose to call artistic creation a 'System' when
that word is freighted, in Blake, with strongly negative overtones?
Furthermore, are we to take this as Blake's programme or should we
make a distinction? For the words, in the text, seem to be spoken by,
and attributed to, Los, the visionary blacksmith imagined ('created')
by Blake as the artificer of the world of time and space, on the one
hand, and Golgonooza—the city of art—on the other. What is
Blake's relation to his creature Los?

Let me begin with this last question, which is very much the same
question as 'What is the relation of Blake to the works that bear his
name?' In his first four engraved works he comes forward on the
title-page as 'Author & Printer'. But with *The Marriage of Heaven and
Hell* a dramatic change occurs. From that point, every engraved
work except one will make no representation as to authorship.
'Printed by W[illiam] Blake' is the typical formula for what he
called, in a remarkable paradox, his 'consciously . . . Inspired' (*M* 2)
works. Only *Milton*, Blake's one confessedly autobiographical poem,
is by 'The Author & Printer W[illiam] Blake'. These title pages thus
confirm his recurrent statements—both public and private—that
the authors of much of the Blakean canon are 'in Eternity', and that
he is their inspired vehicle.

As a consequence, although first-person 'authorial' voicing can be
traced in many of Blake's works, they are distinguished by a non-
subjective inflection. This situation is perhaps most clearly carried
out—paradoxically—in *Milton*, where Blake appears in propria
persona. As the record of certain particular historical and autobiographical experiences, the poem introduces us first to Blake (the
work's 'Author & Printer') and then to a series of other persons
whom Blake encountered in visionary and non-visionary contexts.

The most notable of these, for our immediate purposes, are the Bard, Los, Milton, and Albion. Each is a distinct individual, but as the poem develops we observe a process of merging and mutual identification.

This process is nicely illustrated in the plot structure of the poem. At the beginning, Blake asks 'what mov'd Milton' to leave 'heav'n' and 'go into the nether deep' in order to redeem himself and his 'Sixfold Emanation'. The answer is 'A Bards prophetic Song', and that song is then transcribed in the text (on plates 3–12/14).[11] Afterwards the 'authorial' narrative re-emerges and continues to the end of the poem. But throughout the work Blake remains as it were 'a character' in his own text, a figure who undergoes experiences and who interacts with the other characters. The consequence is *Milton*'s curiously self-infolded structure of relations: a certain bardic text moves the poet Milton to leave his unhappy heaven, but of course this text is part of Blake's text; furthermore, it is the poet Milton's act of leaving heaven which inspires Blake to his own acts of self-examination and change. And the process replicates itself continually. Ololon, the invention of William Blake, is the emanation of the poet Milton; she inspires Milton to his act of self-transformation and she appears in mortal guise to Blake, who is, like his seventeenth century forebear, unhappy though in the heaven of his life at Felpham under the dominion of the destructive benevolence of Blake's corporeal friend/spiritual enemy William Hayley. Finally, all these acts take place 'in', or as part of, the life-history of 'Albion', and they are to be understood as instances of the work of the 'Eternal Prophet' Los.

Who is doing what to whom in this work? It is a complex question, and a question of exactly the same order as our earlier one about Los and Blake. Not that we have difficulty distinguishing the identities of the various persons—these are clear to us. But that clarity is problematic because, in these strange works, we are continually frustrated in our efforts to connect particular acts with particular persons. The acts that we witness appear as the simultaneous deeds of all the various figures in the text. The time-span of the work *Milton*, we are to understand, is only an instant, 'a pulsation of the artery' (*M* 28: 47), though its empirical history stretches at least from the early seventeenth to the early nineteenth centuries.

[11] The discrepancy in the plate-numbers here signals a difference in the ordering of the plates in the different copies.

These complications are the result of one of Blake's most important insights: that the structure of action is exchange or reciprocity, and crucially, that reciprocities—the forms of human causation—are not unidirectional. This insight he then translated into artistic and poetic terms, and it is his acts of translation—the forms he developed—which define the greatness of his work.

Almost any Blakean text would serve for illustration. *The Marriage of Heaven and Hell* is the most spectacular early example, a non-narrative sequence of arrayed textual units where each one replicates the others from a different vantage-point. The whole work is appropriately introduced by the outrageous opening 'Argument', a form which by convention signals the coming of a sequenced narrative and proposes to summarize its events and thereby ease the process of reading. As we know, the 'Argument' of the *Marriage* does none of these things. Its text is cast in the form of a story—the four framed stanzas begin, respectively, with the words 'Once', 'Then', 'Till', and 'Now'—but no history we have ever known corresponds to the eventualities of this text; and least of all does the 'Argument' provide us with a summary of the text it precedes. We are strangers in a stranger land here, caught up in a textual world which dismantles our understanding of 'the' world. 'Rintrah roars & shakes his fires in the burdend air': the first line begins with a word, a name, that no one before ever uttered. It comes to us as if it were a word from an Adamic language.

Such a text thereby develops what one might call a significance rather than a meaning, as if it were a text not to be laid under a process of 'interpretation' but turned towards, listened to, learnt from. It not only speaks as one having some kind of original authority, it speaks as if all authority, all speech, were only significant if possessed of that kind of originality. Neither philology nor allegoresis will be able to unfold the meaning of this work and its epitomizing first word; for this work and its words are formed as communicative actions and not as texts to be deciphered.

The illuminated presentation emphasizes the non-linear character of the material. These are not illustrated poems, they are multiply coded presentations which urge us to grasp verbal and graphic forms simultaneously—as if 'reading' and 'seeing' were to change their conventional roles and objects. The effort of the audience, as a consequence, is primarily devoted to an elemental re-ordering of the faculties in order to permit those transformed actions to take place. Thus the reader of Blake is to approach his work much as Blake imagined anyone would who sought to establish a relationship with the Beloved he called Truth. The relationship can only be founded on an entire opening of the doors of perception. Such a commitment, which amounts to a decision toward utter self-abandonment, is reciprocated by the 'notice' of 'truth' herself—a notice which confirms the decision to self-abandonment, a notice which, like the judgement of every Beloved, delivers the lover over to a withering critical judgement of his limits and inadequacies.

Blake's work thus deters us from carrying out facile interpretative translations, those thematic resolutions which suggest that we know the Truth (rather than that the Truth knows us). The work builds structures that resist consumption in the meta-physics of 'opinion' and 'ideology'. The conceptual transformations Blake wants to effect are set in motion at the primary levels of experience—at 'physical' rather than 'meta-physical' levels, at the very 'doors of perception'. For the errors of the mind are here grasped as errors of perception— literally, errors of the *body* of what and how we know or think we know. This procedure shares something in common with the 'aesthesis' attributed to poetry by the Kantian tradition. But the difference is even more striking and important: that a Blakean 'aesthesis' is to conduct one not to centres of indifference, still points, or balance and reconciliation, it is toward social and psychic over- throw.

The initial entry into Blake's work has, therefore, to be along biblio-graphical lines because these direct us to pay attention to the physique of the work and its institutions of production and re- production. The grammatology of his inventions proceeds as a de- scriptive anatomy. This seems very clear, for example, when we try to negotiate the opening sections of *Milton* and its presentation of the Bard's Song and Milton's 'unexampled deed'. To the question of 'what mov'd Milton' the text replies as follows:

> A Bards prophetic Song! for sitting at eternal tables,
> Terrific among the Sons of Albion in chorus solemn & loud
> A Bard broke forth! all sat attentive to the awful man.
>
> Mark well my words! they are of your eternal salvation;
> Three Classes are Created by the Hammer of Los, & Woven

> *A Bards prophetic Song: for sitting at eternal tables,*
> *Terrific among the Sons of Albion in chorus solemn & loud*
> *A Bard broke forth! all sat attentive to the awful man.*
>
> *Mark well my words! they are of your eternal salvation;*
>
> *Three Classes are Created by the Hammer of Los, & Woven*

This is the way the Bard's song begins at the end of plate 3. A textual crux is created by the presence of two visual interruptions: the interlinear ornaments between the third and the fourth lines here, and the extra spacing between the fourth and the fifth created by Blake's excision of a line from the copperplate. The problem is to determine at what line the song actually begins: do we take 'Mark well my words! they are of your eternal salvation' as the opening line of the Bard's song, or is it an 'authorial' direction, part of the initial passage which we have been hearing, to this point, as the voice of 'The Author & Printer W. Blake'?

Through the course of the Bard's song the problematic line appears as a refrain—repeated four times in copies A and B, and five (and a half) times in copies C and D. Those subsequent uses do not settle the question of assignment. Indeed, in one instance—the so-called plate *a* in copies C and D—the problem is exacerbated because the line is not spaced out in the text, as it is in every other case. The plate *a* passage occurs in the course of the opening speech of Los: this is the way the text appears:

> Beneath the Plow of Rintrah & the Harrow of the Almighty
> In the hands of Palamabron. Where the Starry Mills of Satan
> Are built beneath the Earth & Waters of the Mundane Shell
> Here the Three Classes of Men take their Sexual texture Woven
> The Sexual is Threefold: the Human is Fourfold.
>
> If you account it Wisdom when you are angry to be silent, and
> Not to shew it: I do not account that Wisdom but Folly.
> Every Mans Wisdom is peculiar to his own Individ[u]ality
> O Satan my youngest born, art thou not Prince of the Starry Hosts
> And of the Wheels of Heaven, to turn the Mills day & night?
> Art thou not Newtons Pantocrator weaving the Woof of Locke
> To Mortals thy Mills seem every thing & the Harrow of Shaddai
> A Scheme of Human conduct invisible & incomprehensible
> Get to thy Labours at the Mills & leave me to my wrath.
>
> Satan was going to reply, but Los roll'd his loud thunders.

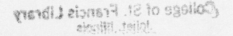

Beneath the Plow of Rintrah & the Harrow of the Almighty
In the hands of Palamabron. Where the Starry Mills of Satan
Are built beneath the Earth & Waters of the Mundane Shell
Here the Three Classes of Men take their Sexual texture Woven
The Sexual is Threefold: the Human is Fourfold

If you account it Wisdom when you are angry to be silent, and
Not to shew it: I do not account that Wisdom but Folly.
Every Mans Wisdom is peculiar to his own Individuality
O Satan my youngest born, art thou not Prince of the Starry Hosts
And of the Wheels of Heaven, to turn the Mills day & night,
Art thou not Newtons Pantocrator weaving the Woof of Locke
To Mortals thy Mills seem every thing & the Harrow of Shaddai
A scheme of Human conduct invisible & incomprehensible
Get to thy Labours at the Mills & leave me to my wrath.

Satan was going to reply, but Los rolld his loud thunders.

Anger me not! thou canst not drive the Harrow in pitys paths.
Thy Work is Eternal Death, with Mills & Ovens & Cauldrons.
Trouble me no more. thou canst not have Eternal Life

So Los spoke! Satan trembling obeyd weeping along the way.
Mark well my words, they are of your eternal Salvation

Between South Molton Street & Stratford Place: Calvarys foot
Where the Victims were preparing for Sacrifice their Cherubim
Around their loins pourd forth their arrows & their bosoms beam
With all colours of precious stones, & their innmost palaces
Resounded with preparation of animals wild & tame
(Mark well my words! Corporeal Friends
    are Spiritual Enemies)

Mocking Druidical Mathematical
Proportion of Length Bredth Highth
Displaying Naked Beauty! with Flute &
Harp & Song

Anger me not! thou canst not drive the Harrow in pitys paths.
Thy Work is Eternal Death, with Mills & Ovens & Cauldrons.
Trouble me no more. thou canst not have Eternal Life

So Los spoke! Satan trembling obeyed weeping along the way.
Mark well my words, they are of your eternal salvation

Between South Molton Street & Stratford Place: Calvarys foot
Where the Victims were preparing for Sacrifice their Cherubim
Around their loins pourd forth their arrows & their bosoms beam
With all colours of precious stones, & their inmost palaces
Resounded with preparation of animals wild & tame
(Mark well my words! Corporeal Friends are Spiritual Enemies)
Mocking Druidical Mathematical Proportion of Length Bredth Highth
Displaying Naked Beauty! with Flute & Harp & Song

(MILTON plate 4, lines 1–28, Copy D)

Here the untypical positioning of the refrain-line may be taken as a
signal to assign it, in this case, to Los. We may not in the end be so
certain about such an assignment, but the typography generates an
association of the line with Los that recuperates the initial ambiguity
of association.

I have set out this long passage from plate 4 because it illustrates
an important and related typographical problem in Blake's work:
his refusal to employ either single or double quotation-marks to
distinguish the speaking voices in his texts. This refusal is not
peculiar to the present work, it is typical of them all. In only two
cases—both occur in *The [First] Book of Urizen*—does Blake supply
inverted commas to mark off a speaker. In the present instance, the
absence of quotation-marks, coupled with the irregular spacing of
the verses and the appearance of interlinear ornamental breaks,
introduces a reading problem into the text. The dysfunction appears
initially at line 9, when we discover that a voice has entered the text
without our having been aware of it.

That discovery generates a further textual crux if we try to determine when precisely Los had begun to speak in the text. Retro-
spectively we may decide, as most editors of Blake have decided,
that Los began speaking at line 6; and we may then enshrine that
decision by 'editing' Blake's text as many have done, that is, by
supplying the 'appropriate' inverted commas. That process of editing
would prevent the arrival of Blake's textual dysfunction and, in a
certain respect, 'clarify' the text. But such a 'clarifying' process

creates a dysfunction of its own by preventing one of Blake's most typical effects: forcing readers to revise continually their perceptions of things.

Reading Blake's unedited text, in this particular case, goes through a typical three-stage Blakean process as one moves from a point of initial ignorance, by way of an awareness of ambiguity, to a subsequent (but not final) state of understanding, where, however, those first two moments of the experience are not removed. That 'failure' to remove the earlier stages of the textual experience is entirely positive, is indeed the very heart of the procedure. In the passage we are now examining, line 19 is our first explicit signal that Los has been speaking in the text, and we could retrace our reading-steps to try to decide when he began; but we could not, even after such a retracing, take back either the blinded experience (when we did not realize there was an ambiguity at all) or the problematic experience (when we registered the initial dysfunction). But Blake does not want us to erase those dialectical moments, or even gather them under an illusory synthesis. These moments are to preserve their particular identities for ever, so that—as Blake will commonly say—not one moment of time or space should be lost (e.g. *M* 20: 19–20).

We note on *Milton*, plate 4, another quite typical form in which Blake manipulates his texts for these kinds of effect. I have in mind here the problem of line 21; for after the experience of lines 1–19, the reader will encounter line 21 with some hesitation about how to read it. If the refrain-line (20) gets associated with Los, we shall be even more inclined to consider line 21 as a continuation of Los's words to Satan. Gradually, as we read on, we may allow the text to subside into the Bard's song, and no longer assign the words to any particular character presented through that song. But the delayed understanding cannot undo the previous imaginations which the text has generated. For in Blake, uncertainties, and even misunderstandings, are as full of truth as comprehensions and 'firm persuasions'.

Blake manages such effects by managing the graphic presentation of his text. In this case we have been focusing on the elementary importance of one of his recurrent (un)conventions, the absence of quotation-marks. But we have to note as well the way Blake uses line-spacing to unpunctuate his texts even further. The ambiguities on plates 3 and 4 of *Milton*, get generated through the interaction of the spacing with the unpunctuation.

Plate 3 illustrates, in addition, how the plate-structure of these works can contribute to their textual peculiarities. In this instance, our uncertainty about where the Bard's song begins—fundamentally, our uncertainty about the formal relation of that song to 'Blake's' poem—is reinforced because the problematic lines come in at the foot of the plate. The line 'Three Classes are Created by the Hammer of Los, & Woven' is so positioned as to suspend even further our attempt to grasp its rhetorical structure. Like the spaced-out refrain-line, it too hangs alone for a moment, disconnected from the text that precedes it and the text that follows.

Under the circumstances, we may come to see in the refrain-line a typically Blakean kind of self-referential word-play. We are to pay close attention to the words of this text, but that attention will here necessarily involve trying to mark out the text's punctuation, and thereby both its grammar and form. We shall, in the event, have to 'Mark well' the problem of such minute particulars as the pro-nominal references of 'my' and 'your' in the refrain-line; and we shall have to consider how such an apparently insignificant textual issue could be connected to anyone's 'eternal salvation'.

IV

Let me now try to run back over the series of questions posed in this chapter. On the matter of the relation of Blake to Los, we see in *Milton* that the two are made poetic transforms of each other. In the paradoxical formulation arrived at in *Jerusalem*, these transforms are to be 'identified' (*J* 99: 1–2), are to be seen as a single 'Divine Appearance' (*J* 96: 7) within which various particular individuals will be distinguished in 'likeness & similitude' (*J* 96: 7, 22). The identifications, founded at the textual level, epitomize the poetry's general 'system' of transformations we traced in the opening section of *Milton*, that is, in the plates carrying us to the end of the Bard's song. There we observe the multiple references opened to those nervous pronouns in the refrain-line. 'My' may be taken, by the end of the song, as any one of the characters named in the text 'Author & Printer', 'the Bard', or 'Milton'; and 'your' may be any of these figures as well as some others, including anyone reading the work. By the conclusion of the poem the transformations will have been multiplied even further. *Milton*, for example, like *Vala* before and *Jerusalem* after, is in some sense the expressed form of the dream of the sleeping Albion; and since both 'Bard' and 'Author & Printer' produce their work under a confessed inspiration, we have to listen for the eternal authority that speaks through the text, including the text of the Bard's song. That authority is, *in some sense*, also to be 'identified' with figures like Leutha, Ololon, Jesus. For 'the Divine Voice [is] heard in [all] the Songs of Beulah' (*M* 32: 1), including the Bard's Song, which is one of those songs.

This system of transformations is well known to Blake scholars. More recent work has begun to show how that system is not so much a 'myth' or conceptual structure—which are the forms elaborated through so much Blake criticism—as it is a function of the work's rhetorical orders in their material actuality. '[T]he Writing|Is the Divine Revelation in the Litteral expression' (*M* 44: 13–14). Blake emphasizes the literalness of such work because he wants the text to collapse the (philosophical) distinction between signifier and signified. In a linguistic system where words have become things, the referential order is transformed into a set of prescribed (but not *prescriptive*) activities. These texts are designed to 'move' the reader much as Milton, and Blake, were moved to 'unexampled deed[s]' of their own. The 'reference-level' of the text is therefore not to some 'world', whether known, 'real', or even imagined. It is not 'to' anything at all. Blake's poetry rather looks 'towards', calls out 'to', reciprocal forms of activity—acts which are 'unexampled' in the previous experience of the authors of those acts, 'Blake's' 'audience'.

Althusser would have said that such poetry 'interpellates' its audience. And Althusser would therefore have been obliged to say that Blake's work is not art but propaganda—a bastard form of art enmeshed in the illusions of ideology. For Althusser, as for philosophy in general since Kant, art was to be set aside from those struggles of truth and error that get carried out in the continuing engagements between science, on one hand, and ideology on the other. Art's place in those struggles was rather to uphold an ideal of coherence and order, to preserve that ideal as the ultimate goal in the struggles for truth. Poetry would be the still point in a furiously turning world.

For Blake, however, such a view relegated poetry to a memorial function, and turned imagination into the faculty which produces images of the best that has been known and thought in the world. Furthermore, it represented the struggle for truth as (quite literally) a non-imaginative one—as a struggle, carried out in the wastelands of morality, between the priests and the pragmatists, between the prescriptive and the demonstrative reasoners. Poetry was to offer another form of truth altogether.

Briefly, Blake did not see truth as a 'correspondence' to some presumed or hypothesized 'reality', whether 'externalist' or 'internalist', nor even as an arbitrary set of formal or intratextual correspondences. Blakean truth resembles Putnam's 'internalist' truth because Blake does not believe that truth exists objectively. Truth for Blake does not *exist*, it has to be created. Once it is brought into being, however, Blakean truth immediately discovers—calls attention to—its own precise and objective limits. He defined the process of truth-creation very early, and presented it explicitly in *The Marriage of Heaven and Hell* as the dialectic of Prolific and Devourer. The typical perversion of this process, also set out in the *Marriage*, is the refusal to recognize 'the bound and outward circumference' which energetic acts define for themselves; Blake calls that perversion casting 'poetic tales' into 'forms of worship'.

But what I have just given is no more than a schema of Blake's 'system' of truth. The *truth* of Blake's poetry emerges as the textual 'performances' of his imaginative communications. Blake's 'system' 'creates' the conditions whereby those communicative acts 'giv[e] a body to Falshood that it may be cast off for ever' (*J* 12:13). It is a 'system' of 'Adverse wheels' where expenses of energy expose and define the limits of the energy expended. Blake usually saw it in architectural terms, a project designed to erect what he called 'Buildings of Los[s]'. In specular terms, we might say that every picture of the world assumes a point of view—Blake imagined it as a vortex—which discovers the limits of that picture; and Blake would go on to show that those limits, in their body of falsehoods, establish the terms within which the transcendence of those limits becomes possible. Both vortex and transcendence therefore assume definite, material, and limited forms. For every transcendence will be (correctly) seen, from any (and every) other point of view, as another form of error.

Blake's new anatomy of truth, therefore, is actually a set of directions for how to deal with falsehood and error. In this respect, Blake's is much closer to a Socratic (which is not to say a Platonic) form of truth than to anything else. But because Blake came to grips with the problem of truth as a practising artist, rather than as an academic or a philosopher, his philosophical significance is to be sought, and defined, in his graphic and poetical work, and not in his

ideas as such. Blake's radical swerve from the Kantian line of
aesthetics, which was emerging at the same time, involves precisely
his argument that art and imagination have more to do with truth
and falsehood than do all forms of 'abstract reasoning', whether
'priestly' or 'natural'. Blake's poetry is an illumination of the literal
truth.

Blake's poetry is 'true' because, in his typical practice, it executes
a more comprehensive definition of the mind's activies than do other
types of human discourse. Unlike philosophical or scientific work,
poetic forms do not seek to establish those many types of abstract
control (categories, rules, methodologies, etc.) which are necessary
to science, history, philosophy. On the contrary, the only 'rule' of
poetic work is that it develop as rich a field of concretions and
details, as complex a network of relations (similarities and differences
alike) as can be imagined. This diversity is established through what
Blake called 'the bounding line', along which 'minute particulars'
achieve their distinctnesses. What emerges from that field is what a
historicist would see as the 'context', more or less complete depending
on the excellence of the work, wherein the activities are carried out.

Crucial to Blake's work is his understanding that art solicits error,
without which there can be no possibility of truth. For Blake, error
does not enter the imagination inadvertently, or by mistake, as it
does in other forms of discourse. It enters by the will, deliberately,
though that will may not necessarily be a conscious one. When
Blake observed that 'There can be no Good Will Will is always Evil'
(*Ann. to Swed: Love*), he was glancing at what we should call the
ideology of art, and the way ideology enters imaginative work. For
Blake held that poetry had to embrace the conflicts of good and evil,
had in fact to generate those conflicts. So Blake's anatomy of truth
always emerges as a body of falsehood. Will turns the Satanic wheel
which, in poetic discourse, is meshed in a more complex system of
other and 'adverse' wheels—wheels that are contraries, wheels that
are contradictions, wheels that are 'within' and wheels that are
'without'. Arching above this self-destructive system of Evil human
will, above the 'Eternal Death' which the system generates, is what
Blake named 'the World of Eternity' under whose illumination the
work of imagination gets carried out.

One immediate consequence of Blake's radical redefinition of
poetry's relation to truth is that his own work displays its wilfulness,
and hence its errors, on its many faces. Some of these errors are

already clear to us: the sexist structure of his thought, for example, or the crudely fetishized parodies of dialectical thinking which enter his work, especially after 1803, via his Christianity. Others could easily be remarked. Myself, I think particularly of his repeated insistence that in imagination nothing is ever lost, that every particular of time and space is preserved for-ever. In *Milton*, for example, Blake, 'posses'd' by the 'Shadowy Prophet' Los, declares:

> I in Six Thousand Years walk up and down; for not one Moment
> Of Time is lost, nor one event of Space unpermanent
> But all remain
>
> $(M\ 20:\ 18–20)^{12}$

This seems to me a wilful distortion of the truth in an effort to supply what is ultimately a Christian consolation for the losses we suffer and endure. Entropy is not an idea which Blake's mind would have entertained, just as he cannot think of a hell that is no part of a redemptive process: 'Every moment lost, is a moment that cannot be redeemed' (*J* 77). Seen more positively, there is nothing in his mind which will not *serve*, no voice that is permitted to speak an ultimate Satanic refusal.

Blake's will toward a complete redemptive scheme opens an important gap in his work—a kind of meta-absence, the refusal of that Satanic principle which Coleridge called 'positive negation', and which the nineteenth century in general feared and sought to banish. The most dramatic instance of Blake refusing refusal appears in the central drama of *Jerusalem*, when Albion collapses into despair:

> Hark! the mingling cries of Luvah with the Sons of Albion.
> Hark! & Record the terrible wonder! that the Punisher
> Mingles with his Victims Spectre, enslaved and tormented
> To him whom he has murderd, bound in vengeance & enmity
> Shudder not, but Write, & the hand of God will assist you!
> Therefore I write Albions last words, Hope is banish'd from me.

> These were his last words, and the merciful Saviour in his arms
> Reciev'd him, in the arms of tender mercy and repos'd
> The pale limbs of his Eternal Individuality
> Upon the Rock of Ages.
>
> $(J\ 47:\ 12–17,\ 48:\ 1–4)$

---

12 See also *J* 13: 60, 75: 7–9.

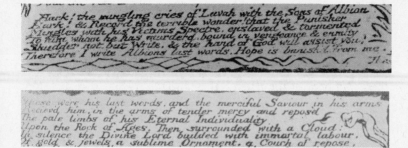

It is a splendid text in which we observe that characteristic Blakean transformation-process, whereby the actions of 'the merciful Saviour' merge into, get identified with, the act of Blake's poem, into whose 'arms of tender mercy' Albion is here received. Albion's despair is no other than his way into Eternal Death, his self-victimization. We are to understand, therefore, that even as Albion loses all hope, his redemption has finally entered a positive phase.

To such representations the critical mind will simply say, 'If you *will* believe that, you will believe anything.' And Blake will be ready with his reply, which is: that his entire work is produced in order to restore the mind to belief, to generate a faithful imagination. This was a message which he repeated tirelessly throughout his creative life.

But we are left, through Blake's own work, either to belief or to disbelief on this question. This happens because Blake himself is not completely faithful, though he would like to be. There are many political, moral, and social ideas which he does not believe and could not imagine—which *in fact* fell outside his work's redemptive schemes—but the most telling absence of all is his disbelief in, his inability to imagine, a sin against the light. Dante, the Bible, and even Milton were able to imagine that sin; Blake was not. And he was not because he was, despite himself, an illuminist—bound to his victim, eighteenth-century deism, which (dis)appeared once again into that ultimate condition of transformation and absentia, Blake's illuminated work.

Yet the traces of Blake's failures of imagination are preserved in all his work—'redeemed', if you will, according to the law of the ideology he himself embraced. In this respect Blake innovated an important artistic method for revealing what is true. His work therefore stands in witness against itself; but it does this obliquely, at what Emily Dickinson called a 'slant'. The 'Evil' which Blake defined as an absence[13] is not *present* to Blake as it is, for example, to Dante, who adhered to a similar (in his case, a Thomistic) concept of evil as negation. In Blake the negation is negated, what is absent is not there. But because the *absence is* there, what is missing rises up before us as what has been rejected by imagination, rises up as the absent reality—rises up, finally, as objectivity and otherness, without which imagination must become a hollow idea rather than what it is, a form of human action.

In this way Blake illuminated the truth. For absences spring from human interests, from the acts of directed beings, from the (for Blake, false) will to truth. In this way absences structure the conditions for a renewal of presence. But in Blake the structure is of a very particular kind, and it shows—despite itself—that the renewal will never be complete: for there is always, objectively, more adversity than may be returned on the 'Adverse Wheel' of Blake's or any other poet's verse. Nothing shows this so well as plate 3 of *Jerusalem*, the text on which I began this discussion.

The plate illuminates the truth—literally, the texts that are present and the texts that have been removed. Through the labour and expertise of scholars like David Erdman, most of the gouged parts of the plate have been recovered. These restorations are not complete, however, and some remain frankly conjectural. Their loss to us is an exponent of the kind of knowledge we have, and of the kind of knowledge we shall always have. Blake's illuminated text, on the other hand, demonstrates the human agencies and frameworks through which our knowledge is constituted. The plate is an obvious comment on the limits of knowledge, but it is also a self-reflexive illumination of the whole truth about *Jerusalem*: that it is incommensurate with itself.

We may take this, I think, as an emblem of Blake's deepest insight into the truth of which artistic work is capable. By representing absence so dramatically, Blake admits the limits of his work, admits the limits of imagination itself—in the end, even begins to *imagine* the ideology of imagination.

That is an imagination which cultural studies have been resisting for almost two hundred years. During that time we have decided,

[13] See his Annotations to Lavater (E 601).

after Keats, that what the imagination seizes as beauty must be truth. But we have tended to read Keats's text too narrowly, as if it rendered unthinkable certain contradictory ideas. Assenting to Keats's statement does *not*, however, mean that we cannot also assent to the following statements:

> what the imagination seizes as beauty may be false;
> what the imagination seizes as ugliness may be truth.

Romantic theory is not comfortable with such thoughts or such imaginations. Indeed, Blake himself tended to shrink away from them, as one may readily see from the mutilated plate 3 of *Jerusalem*, where Blake's final artistic effort—the application of the water-colours—gracefully mutes the damage he inflicted at the earlier stage of production.

Perhaps readers are mistaken, then, when they read this plate under the sign of melancholia. Certainly the plate itself, *as illuminated*, deals serenely with its own damaged parts. But if we think Blake was wrong to have covered his sins here so beautifully, we may also think—may we not?—that hypocrisy often puts on a saving face. It was a thought that occurred to Blake often enough.

CHAPTER 2

Lord Byron's Twin Opposites of Truth

Lift your weapons. Here is the one that resists intentions.

CLARK COOLIDGE, *The Crystal Text*

SINCERITY: that is one of the key touchstones by which Romantic poetry originally measured itself.[1] In a poem's sincerity one observed a deeply felt relation binding the poetic Subject to the poetic subject, the speaking voice to the matter being addressed. That veritable proverb of Romanticism—'Everything is as it is perceived'—simply translates the idea of sincerity into phenomenological terms. It is a maxim reminding us of the truth-structure postulated by the idea, and the style, of sincerity: that the 'truth' of something is a function of one's belief or imagination. Romantic truth is inner vision, and Romantic knowledge is the unfolding of the truths of that inner vision.

Hypocrisy is the antithesis of sincerity. One can be sincere and yet speak incompletely, inadequately, or even falsely, but it appears a patent contradiction to think or imagine that one could be sincere and at the same time speak deliberate falsehoods or develop subtle equivocations. To do so is to declare that one is 'two-faced', and hence lacking that fundamental quality of the sincere person: integrity.

This absence of integrity has its own special dynamism and positivities, however. Lying and hypocrisy require attention, artfulness, intelligence—as Scott so memorably reminds us:

> O, what a tangled web we weave,
> When first we practise to deceive!
>
> (*Marmion*, VI, st. 17)

Discourse is sincere, in a Romantic mode, when it appears least

---

[1] For two good generic discussions of sincerity in Romanticism see David Perkins, *Wordsworth and the Poetry of Sincerity* (Cambridge, Mass., 1964); Lionel Trilling, *Sincerity and Authenticity* (Cambridge, Mass., 1972).

concerned with the effect it produces. Thus we recognize the style of sincerity by its self-attention (some would add, by its self-absorption). Of such a poetry we say, following John Stuart Mill, that it is not to be 'heard' but 'overheard'.

In this respect Romantic poetry presents itself as artless and unpremeditated, a poetry carried out in the theatre of the self, whence others, though they have not been solicited, will not be expelled if they happen or determine to be there. The poetry of sincerity appears to shrink from rhetoric, audience-manipulation, and self-display. Postulating an ideal of self-knowledge, such poetry seeks after a world of perfect epistemological clarity.

In this context of thought, rhetorical and premeditated verse may be imagined prima facie incapable with respect to truth and knowledge. Furthermore, hypocrisy will be judged to arise as a possibility just when discourse (including poetic discourse) is self-consciously directed beyond itself to an audience which has been precognized in some explicit way, which is assumed to be present, and which is directly addressed. The poetry of sincerity—Romantic poetry, in its paradigm mode—therefore typically avoids the procedures of satirical and polemical verse. Those latter forms—by their protocols—develop through publically installed dialogical operations. When Romantic poetry opens itself to those genres it opens itself to the horizon of its antithesis, to the horizon of hypocrisy.[2]

This last move is, of course, exactly what Byron did. We should not be surprised, then, that he is the one English Romantic who has been commonly charged with—who has had his work charged with—hypocrisy.[3] This consequence reflects an important and (if I may so phrase it) two-faced fact about Byron as a writer: that he cultivated

[2] Romantic drama—for example, the drama of Coleridge, Shelley, or Byron—presents a special case of Romantic absorption. No literary mode is more socialized than the drama: this is a historical and an institutional fact which declares itself in the relation which persists between theatre and drama. The development of 'closet drama'—which is what happened in Romanticism—clearly breaks down that relationship, or at least throws it into a crisis. The separation of the drama from the theatre is an index of Romanticism itself.

[3] The charge was first raised in the controversy over Byron's 'Poems on his Domestic Circumstances', and particularly in relation to 'Fare Thee Well!' John Gibson Lockhart's comment on Don Juan—'Stick to Don Juan: it is the only sincere thing you have ever written' (quoted in Andrew Rutherford (ed.), Byron: The Critical Heritage (New York, 1970), 183)—nicely captures the problem of Byron's sincerity, for that view exactly flew in the face of the dominant line of contemporary criticism. The latter would have been able to say much the same thing that Lockhart said, only for Don Juan it would have substituted Childe Harold.

rhetorical modes of verse, and that *he was a Romantic poet who cultivated those modes*. The distinction is crucial. We do not always remember, for instance, that the touchstones of Romanticism point towards styles of writing rather than states of mind or soul—that 'sincerity' in poetry is an illusion generated by the way certain forms of language have been deployed. We do not remember this because we have inherited so much of the Romantic aesthetic that we often (un-willingly and unconsciously) suspend our disbelief in that aesthetic. But Byron, and Byron's poetry, never forgets for very long the provisional and rhetorical character of what he and it are doing. When Byron suspends his disbelief (or his belief) in his writing, he does so with a will and with extreme self-consciousness.

Hypocrisy may therefore be seen as the measure of the importance of Byron's work. It is the dark double of Romantic sincerity, the one 'truth' of Romanticism which it appeared unable to imagine. It fell to Byron, however, to reveal through his own work the larger truth of Romanticism: that its 'sincerity', its 'imagination', its 'true voice of feeling' are all constructs erected for various particular purposes and reasons. *Don Juan* is a machine for exposing many kinds of hypocrisy—cant political, cant poetical, cant moral, Byron called them—and there is no one, I suppose, who would gainsay the extraordinary scale of Byron's achievement. Nevertheless, what we have still to see more clearly is how this satire of hypocrisy is grounded in Byron's Romanticism, and how the latter is the very seat and primal scene of what it means to be hypocritical. In the end we shall discover a poetic truth-function which Byron, alone of the English Romantics, elaborated and deployed. An essential feature of this work is the understanding that hypocrisy and the true voice of feeling cannot be separated (even if they can be distinguished). Paradoxical though it may seem, this is a discovery which may be imagined with peculiar—perhaps unexampled—clarity through the styles of Romanticism.

At the heart of the Romantic ideal of sincerity are two related problems, the one a contradiction, the other an illusion. The contra-diction is concealed in the Romantic Idea(l) of self-integrity. Byron summed up this problem with great wit and trenchancy:

> Also observe, that like the great Lord Coke,
>   (See Littleton) whene'er I have expressed
> Opinions two, which at first sight may look
>   Twin opposites, the second is the best.

Perhaps I have a third too in a nook,
        Or none at all—which seems a sorry jest;
But if a writer would be quite consistent,
How could he possibly show things existent?

(xv, st. 87)[4]

This anticipates exactly the critique of the Romantic idea(l) of subjectivity that would be raised so powerfully by Kierkegaard in his analysis of Hegel's paradigmatic representation of the truth-content of that ideal. Kierkegaard's 'Concluding Unscientific Post-script' ridicules the 'German philosopher'—'Herr Professor'—for the abstraction of Hegel's concept of subjective and phenomenological truth, which cannot be 'realized for any existing spirit, who is himself existentially in process of becoming'.[5]

I will summarize briefly Kierkegaard's argument on this matter because it helps to clarify the import and structure of Byron's poetical work. According to Hegel, the idea(l) of identity is a dialectical synthesis of 'Twin opposites'. It is achieved when Otherness, that which is not the subject, is 'negated' in the process of knowledge we call consciousness. The objective knowledge that is gained is not positive but phenomenological: not particular subjective or empirical truths, but the metaphysical truth of the process itself.

To this position Kierkegaard raised a simple but devastating problem—his famous *enten—eller*, the 'either/or'. Assuming (with Hegel and the entire metaphysical tradition) the principle of identity, Kierkegaard argued as follows: either the truth that is achieved is identical with consciousness, or it is not truth. If the process is the truth, the process is solipsistic (it involves mere tautologies); if it is not solipsistic, contradiction—untruth—remains part of the process. The 'negation' that is part of the Hegelian process is either the phantom of a negation or a true negation; in the first instance it may be transcended, in the second it may not, but in either case knowledge and truth remain unachieved.

A writer, therefore, cannot 'possibly show things existent' and at the same time 'be consistent'. This contradiction operates because the 'process' of subjectivity is an existential and not a logical (or dialectical) process. Kierkegaard's lively prose style is itself an

---

[4] *Lord Byron. The Complete Poetical Works*, ed. Jerome J. McGann (Oxford, 1980–) v. 614. All quotations from the poetry will be from this edition.
[5] Søren Kierkegaard, *Concluding Unscientific Postscript*, trans. Walter Lowrie (Princeton, 1941), 171.

'existential' critique of German philosophical discourse, a revelation of what it actually means to 'show things existent'. But in this respect the English poet's verse far surpasses the Danish philosopher's arguments:

> If people contradict themselves, can I
>   Help contradicting them, and every body,
> Even my veracious self?—But that's a lie;
>   I never did so, never will—how should I?
> He who doubts all things, nothing can deny.
>
> (xv, st. 88)

The lines enact the contradictions they confront. In this passage Byron at once asserts and denies his self-integrity. His contradiction of himself is a lie, the lines declare, but they also declare that his 'veracious self' is a lie, and hence they equally give the lie to his denial of his self-contradiction.

The passage, in short, turns itself into an illustration, or an instance, of the problem it is proposing to deal with. It is Byron's poetic, 'existential' equivalent of the logical paradox of the lying Cretan. Byron's verse here proposes such a paradox, but it includes its own activity of making the proposal within the paradox, as yet another face of the contradiction.

Later we shall inquire more deeply into the matter of *Don Juan*'s contradictions, but in order to do that we need to understand better the illusions which correspond to those contradictions. If a contradiction exposes itself at the core of Romantic self-integrity, we confront an illusion in the Romantic idea(l) of spontaneity and artlessness. Romantic sincerity only *presents itself* as unpremeditated verse; in fact it involves a rhetoric, and contractual bonds with its audiences, which are just as determinate and artful as the verse of Donne, or Rochester, or Pope. The rhetoric of sincerity in Romanticism is a rhetoric of displacement; the audience is not addressed directly, it is set apart, like the reflective poet himself, in a position where the discourse of the poem has to be overheard. Among the important consequences of this basic manœuvre is the illusion of freedom which it fosters—as if the reader were not being placed under the power of the writer's rhetoric, as if the writer were relatively indifferent to the reader's presence and intent only on communing with his own soul.

In this context, Byron's work is significant precisely to the extent that it deploys its rhetoric of sincerity in highly resistant poetic forms. His most important poetry, as everyone knows, is not carried out in a lyrical mode—this in sharp contrast to all the other Romantics, with the exception of Blake. As a consequence, Byron's work and his audiences always tend to foster a clarity of presence toward each other. This remains true even when he is working in the lyrical form. In general, it is as if Byron in his work were not simply meditating in public, but were declaring or even declaiming his inmost thoughts and feelings out loud, and directly to others. (The procedure has been aptly described as 'trailing his bleeding heart across Europe'.) The difference from the usual romantic practice is crucial. To plumb the significance of that difference will help us measure the truth-functions of a literature (or of a criticism, for that matter) which establishes epistemological clarity and self-knowledge as co-ordinate imperatives of their aesthetic programmes.

II

The first important publication in Byron's career as a poet was a text which he did not write himself, though he had provoked it. I mean Henry Brougham's notorious review of Byron's juvenile *Hours of Idleness* (1807). The article is a shrewd reading of Byron's book, whose marks of vanity and pretentiousness Brougham acutely registers. In addition to ridiculing the technical and stylistic weaknesses of the work, Brougham draws particular attention to the way the book emphasizes Byron's aristocracy on the one hand, and his youth on the other, and he speculates whether Byron might not have a design upon the reader: 'Perhaps . . . all that he tells us about his youth is rather with a view to increase our wonder, than to soften our censures.'[6] Brougham's supercilious contempt for Byron's book never explicitly says that *Hours of Idleness* is the work of a pretentious fool who had miscalculated his ability to manipulate his audience. Nevertheless, this is the point he means to make, as we see in the following passage:

the noble author is peculiarly forward in pleading his minority. We have it in the title-page, and on the very back of the volume; it follows his name like a favourite part of his *style*. Much stress is laid upon it in the preface, and the

---

[6] I take my text of Brougham's review from Rutherford (ed.), *Byron: The Critical Heritage*, 28 (hereafter cited in the text as Rutherford).

poems are connected with this general statement of his case, by particular dates.   (Rutherford, p. 27.)

Brougham is a good reader, not merely of 'the text' in the narrowest conception, but of Byron's *work* here in the largest sense. That is to say, he understands how the texts of Byron's poems are integrated into the format of the book in general. A reading of the individual texts is thereby framed and controlled by various intratextual markers, some of them localized (the 'particular dates' and other such matters referred to by Brougham), and some of them more global (for example, the organization of the book into family and amatory poems, school exercises, and so forth). When Brougham pillories Byron, therefore, it is not so much because the poetry is maudlin or sentimental, as because he detects calculation and insincerity in Byron's book.

English Bards and Scotch Reviewers is Byron's response to—Byron's interpretation of—the textual situation elaborated by Brougham's review. There Brougham 'reads' Byron as if he were not really a serious writer, as if the meaning of his work were to be found in its badly concealed pretences, and—ultimately—in its pretentiousness. *English Bards* is Byron's riposte, his demonstration that he is a serious writer. A critical review of the current state of poetry and British culture generally, the poem mounts for Byron both a self-justification and a self-critique.

The self-justification is clearly if somewhat equivocally made at the start of the poem:

> Still must I hear?—shall hoarse FITZGERALD bawl
> His creaking couplets in a tavern hall
> And I not sing, lest, haply, Scotch Reviews
> Should dub me scribbler, and denounce my Muse?
> Prepare for rhyme—I'll publish, right or wrong:
> Fools are my theme, let Satire be my song.   (1–5)

It is an unusual opening move because Byron does not entirely separate himself from the 'Fools' who are his poem's theme. The touch of recklessness in the determination to 'publish, right or wrong' is fairly paraded in these lines. What Byron gains by that move is an effect of honesty, as if he were—despite his faults as a writer and a person—more candid and morally courageous than those who will be the objects of his satire (that is, bad bards like Fitzgerald and proud reviewers like Brougham).

One notes as well the imperative address to the reader in the fifth line ('Prepare for rhyme'). This manœuvre reminds us of the general literary situation which prevails in Byron's writing even at this stage of his career. The work, that is to say, operates through a textual interplay which is carried out in the public sphere. Byron's two privately printed collections of juvenilia, which predate *Hours of Idleness*, were themselves extremely conscious of their (localized: Southwell and Nottingham) audiences. *Hours of Idleness* is another highly self-conscious book, but in its case the audience is, as we would expect for a *published* text, much more broadly conceived than the two earlier books. Byron tries to manipulate that new audience, and Brougham, its representative at the *Edinburgh Review*, observes the book's designs and ridicules them. The ridicule is a function of the book's efforts to control the audience response, and the review is in part an index that such strategies are at work. But in testifying to the failure of those strategies, the review becomes, in its turn, the occasion through which Byron's writing clarifies itself to itself and reaches for a new level of consciousness.

The special strength of *English Bards* is a function of the Brougham review. Charged by Brougham with insincerity in his earlier book, Byron responds in *English Bards* with a new and more powerful style of sincerity. His polemic is grounded in a significant and daring initial decision: not to deny the charges brought against *Hours of Idleness*. Byron does not even deny Brougham's *ad hominem* critical implications—that Lord Byron, the author of the book, reveals himself in it as a somewhat foolish, calculating, and untrustworthy person.

Byron, in other words, accepts 'sincerity' as the critical issue. Launching an *ad hominem* rejoinder to his Scotch reviewer (who Byron at the time mistakenly thought was Francis Jeffrey) and his critical comrades at the *Edinburgh Review*, Byron admits his weaknesses as a writer and his faults of character. This admission is a new sign of his sincerity, and it is the foundation on which Byron reconstitutes his character in this new poem. *English Bards* argues that Brougham has mistaken his target, that Lord Byron is not the pretentious sentimentalist Brougham took him for.

On the contrary, he is the very figure of youthful courage—impassioned, somewhat reckless, but honest to a fault. His character is displayed equally in his independent pose: he surveys the current literary scene from an apparently disinterested position (he is careful to display his non-alignment with any school or group or even style).

Furthermore, he is not easily intimidated. The Edinburgh reviewers had acquired a fearsome reputation for a kind of brutal candour. When Byron decides to match them strength for strength, therefore, his *figura* of sincerity is even more sharply defined. Byron represents the Scotch reviewers as mere literary bullies—masks of courage—who have been ceded their authority by a timid world which simply refuses to fight back. But now from Byron

> Our men in buckram shall have blows enough,
> And feel, they too are 'penetrable stuff':
> And though I hope not hence unscathed to go,
> Who conquers me, shall find a stubborn foe.   (1049–52)

For his part, 'right or wrong', Byron means to resist, and in taking this position he means as well to construct an image for himself which will set him slightly apart from the 'Fools' who make up the world of Britain.

Being, as he says, the 'least thinking of a thoughtless throng, | Just skilled to know the right and chuse the wrong' (689–90), Byron is a model neither as a poet nor as a 'Moralist' (700). None the less, he refuses to disqualify himself from satire. He has 'learned to think, and sternly speak the truth' (1058), and the truth is that cultural rectitude in Britain has become random and ineffectual—a praise-worthy poet here, a judicious critic there, but none of them—and least of all Lord Byron—installed (or installable) in a position of authority. Byron's poem exposes the lack of a cultural consensus. More than that, it shows how, in the absence of such a consensus, the merely 'righteous' will move to seize such authority.

> Thus much I've dared; if my incondite lay
> Hath wronged these righteous times let others say;   (1067–8)

Lines like these solicit and even glory in their contrariness. At once aggressive and indifferent, the couplet—which concludes the poem—summarizes the tonal character of the satire as a whole, just as it anticipates the tonal perspective of the celebrated writings soon to follow: *Childe Harold* in particular, but all the Baudelairian Oriental tales as well.

The challenge reminds us, however, of the equally important matter we touched on earlier: that the poetry is operating precisely at and as public interchange and discourse. Although Byron shows himself a poet of sincerity in *English Bards*, his peculiar mode of sincerity does not take the form of the internal colloquy. Rather, the

structure of the work is communicative exchange, and this kind of
interplay with the audience will prove a permanent characteristic of
his work. From first to last his books are in direct communication
with the people who are reading them—addressing such people
(often by name) and responding to what they are themselves saying
(as it were) *to* Byron's poems. His work assumes the presence of an
audience that talks and listens—an audience that may hear as well
as overhear, and that may have something to say in its turn.

We recognize this procedure in numerous passages from *Don Juan*:

> Thou shalt believe in Milton, Dryden, Pope;
>> Thou shalt not set up Wordsworth, Coleridge, Southey;
>>> (I, st. 205)

> The other evening ('twas on Friday last)—
>> This is a fact and no poetic fable—
> Just as my great coat was about me cast,
>> My hat and gloves still lying on the table,
> I heard a shot—'twas eight o'clock scarce past—
>> (V, st. 33)

>> My similes are gathered in a heap,
> So pick and chuse—perhaps you'll be content
> With a carved lady on a monument.
>> (VI, st. 68)

The exchange structure is especially interesting when Byron is reflecting upon or responding to criticisms directed at his work by
contemporary readers.

> They accuse me—*Me*—the present writer of
>> The present poem—of—I know not what,—
> A tendency to under-rate and scoff
>> At human power and virtue, and all that;
> And this they say in language rather rough.
>> (VII, st. 3)

> Here I might enter on a chaste description,
>> Having withstood temptation in my youth,
> But hear that several people take exception
>> At the first two books having too much truth;
> Therefore I'll make Don Juan leave the ship soon,
>> Because the publisher declares, in sooth,
> Through needles' eyes it easier for the camel is
> To pass, than these two cantos into families.
>> (IV, st. 97)

Here the act of writing the poetry is clearly making itself one of the principal subjects of the writing. Byron feels free to allude to, or comment upon, almost any part of his literary life—what he did and what came of what he did:

> Oh that I had the art of easy writing
>   What should be easy reading! could I scale
> Parnassus, where the Muses sit inditing
>   Those pretty poems never known to fail,
> How quickly would I print (the world delighting)
>   A Grecian, Syrian, or *Assy*rian tale;
> And sell you, mix'd with western sentimentalism
> Some samples of the finest Orientalism.
>
> *(Beppo, st. 51)*

> In twice five years the 'greatest living poet,'
>   Like to the champion in the fisty ring,
> Is called on to support his claim, or show it,
>   Although 'tis an imaginary thing.
> Even I—albeit I'm sure I did not know it,
>   Nor sought of foolscap subjects to be king,—
> Was reckoned, a considerable time,
> The grand Napoleon of the realms of rhyme.

> But Juan was my Moscow, and Faliero
>   My Leipsic, and my Mont Saint Jean seems
> Cain:
>
> *(Don Juan, XI, sts. 55–6)*

In this kind of work we do not witness simply a poem being written about poetry. That is what we should say, correctly, about much of *The Prelude* or 'The Fall of Hyperion' or a host of other excellent Romantic poems. The situation is slightly but significantly different in Byron's case. Here the act of writing has thoroughly materialized and socialized the field of the imagination's activity. In such circumstances we observe how poetry is like most human events—a dynamic interchange between various parties each of whom plays some part in the total transaction.[7] Those parties are never completely visible or present to consciousness—in Byron's poem or anywhere else; but a poem like *Don Juan*, by calling attention to certain of its com-

---

[7] This is not to suggest that (say) *The Prelude* and 'The Fall of Hyperion' are not themselves just as involved in communicative exchanges as Byron's work; on the contrary, in fact. Byron's work simply foregrounds these exchanges in a clearer way.

municative actions, allows one to glimpse the radical heteronomy of
the exchanges that are taking place.

Byron is quite sensitive to the presence of his many readers—
indeed, his acts of writing are equally acts of imagining them into
existence, and then talking with them. Stanzas 27–32 of *Don Juan*,
Canto I, narrate the marital troubles of Donna Inez and her husband
Don Jóse, but the subtext—the domestic circumstances of Lord and
Lady Byron—exposes the actual structure of Byron's writing here:

> For Inez call'd some druggists and physicians,
>> And tried to prove her loving lord was *mad*,
> But as he had some lucid intermissions,
>> She next decided he was only *bad*;   (st. 27)

And so on. One may read these lines, and the entire passage,
without any knowledge whatever of the autobiographical allusions;
or one may read them with no detailed and particular knowledge,
though with some general sense that personal allusions are being
made; or one may read them from the inside, as it were, as a person
learned in the various references. *Don Juan* has imagined and written
to all three of these audiences.

But it has also done more. The audience of 'knowing ones' (the
phrase is Byron's) is by no means a uniform group. Besides all those
later readers (like ourselves) who are learned in this text by study
and application, the passage has imagined various contemporary
readers. Their presences are helpfully called to our attention through
the surviving proofs of Byron's poem, where two of his readers are
all but materialized for us. The passage above, for example, was
read and annotated by Byron's friend John Cam Hobhouse, who
wrote next to it in the margin of the proof: 'This is so very pointed'.
The comment, one of a series he made in the proofs, was meant to
persuade Byron to moderate various aspects of the satire—for
example, the personal swipes at Lady Byron.[8]

The proofs with Hobhouse's annotations were sent to Byron, who
entered a dialogue with his friend by adding his own marginalia in
response to Hobhouse's strictures. Against the comment of Hobhouse
cited above Byron wrote: 'If people make application it is their own
fault.' Byron's remark is wickedly disingenuous, of course, but it
emphasizes his awareness of 'the people' who might 'make application'

---

[8] The annotations discussed here and below are to be found in the editorial notes
for the relevant passages from *Don Juan* (ed. cit. above, n. 4).

in texts like these. Hobhouse is one of those people—but then so is Lady Byron; and these two readers, equally imagined through this text, will read in very different ways.

This proof material raises two points which I want to emphasize and pursue. First, the 'application' which Hobhouse makes in his reading underscores the variety of *possible* applications: even if we limit the reading group to 'the knowing ones', we can see how differently the passage will be read by Hobhouse, Lady Byron, Augusta Leigh, and so forth. Second, those different readings do not stand outside the text; on the contrary, they are part of the work's imagination of itself. Byron is a reader of his own text here, as his marginal note to Hobhouse indicates. And when we consult the reviews of the first two cantos we find a series of other readers who have been imagined by the writing and who turn upon Byron's texts in various states of outrage, annoyance, disgust. Our later varieties of amusement are to be reckoned up here as well.

Byron's poem, in other words, incorporates a large and diverse group of people into itself. The group includes specific persons, like Hobhouse, Lady Byron, and a host of named or otherwise targeted individuals—literary people (friends, acquaintances, enemies, or simply people he knew or had heard of), politicians, public figures, lovers, and so forth; but it also includes various social, ideological, religious, and political groups (like the bluestockings, the landed aristocracy, the London literary world, the government, the opposition, and a variety of Christian readers). These people are 'in' Byron's poem not simply because they are named or alluded to—not simply at the narratological level—but because Byron's work has called them out—has imagined them as presences at the rhetorical and dialogical levels.

Their responses to the poem, their 'readings', are included in the writing's imagination of itself. We see this very clearly in those passages where Byron appears at his most shocking or tasteless. The parody of the decalogue in Canto I; the scenes of cannibalism, in Canto II; the aftermath of the siege of Ismail when the 'Widows of forty' are made to wonder 'Wherefore the ravishing did not begin!' (VIII, st. 132): these passages horrified early readers, and many of them still retain their offensiveness. The effects are wholly calculated, however, though for certain readers this fact only increases the offence which they represent.

Byron's calculations are meant to draw readers into the orbit of the poem, to insist upon their presence. The stanzas in Canto I (209–10) where Byron declares that he 'bribed my grandmother's review—the British' to write an approving article on *Don Juan* are a good instance of what is happening in Byron's text.

> I sent it in a letter to the editor,
>   Who thank'd me duly by return of post—
> I'm for a handsome article his creditor;
>   Yet if my gentle Muse he please to roast,
> And break a promise after having made it her,
>   Denying the receipt of what it cost,
> And smear his page with gall instead of honey,
> All I can say is—that he had the money.

The allegation is patently outrageous—an amusing poetical flight which calls attention to Byron's general awareness that his poem might cause 'some prudish readers [to] grow skittish'. The editor of *The British Review*, however, William Roberts, took it all in high seriousness, and was moved to issue a public denial of Byron's imaginary declaration. When Byron learned what Roberts had done, he was delighted that one of his most absurd acts of provocation had actually succeeded.[9]

William Roberts is an accomplice in what this text from *Don Juan* carries out. *Don Juan* seeks that kind of complicity, imagines its presence at every point. We laugh at Roberts's foolishness for having risen to Byron's bait here, but the more important matter to grasp is that Roberts's reaction *has to be included in our understanding of Byron's poem*, has to be seen as 'part of' the work. '

Roberts's reaction calls attention to some of the poem's most important discursive procedures. We confront the same kind of situation, for example, when Hobhouse annotates the texts that allude to Lady Byron. Where the poem reads (in reference to Donna Inez and Don Jose):

> She kept a journal, where his faults were noted,
>   And open'd certain trunks of books and letters . . .
>
> (I, st. 28)

the text is glancing at one of Byron's most cherished beliefs about his

---

[9] Byron extended the absurd textual situation by writing a (prose) response to Roberts which he signed 'Wortley Clutterbuck' and published in *The Liberal*. For further details see William H. Marshall, *Byron, Shelley, Hunt and* The Liberal (Philadelphia, 1960), 86–8, 113–14.

wife and her deviousness: 'You know,' Byron wrote to his sister, 'that Lady B[yro]n *secretly opened my letter trunks before she left Town*,'[10] Hobhouse annotates the *Don Juan* lines 'There is some doubt about this', meaning that he is not sure that Lady Byron actually ransacked Byron's belongings in January 1816. What is remarkable here is the *way* Hobhouse is reading, the way he, like Roberts, refuses to distinguish between the fictive and the factive dimensions of the passage. Hobhouse reads the poem as if it were literal statement at the level of the subtext.

Byron's response to Hobhouse's annotation is even more interesting. Against his friend's expression of doubt about the factual truth of Byron's poetic allusion, Byron writes this in the margin:

What has the '*doubt*' to do with the poem? It is at least poetically true—why apply everything to that absurd woman. I have no reference to living characters.

Here disingenuousness unmasks itself as hypocrisy. Byron's argument that his work should not be read outside its purely aesthetic space is belied by his own continual practice. What Byron's remark indicates, however, is his reluctance to accept fully the consequences of the writing-procedures he has set in motion. The writing has collapsed the distinction between factual and fictional space, and it calls various actual readers into its presence. Byron's annotation shows that he still imagines he can control those readers, that he still imagines it is his poetic privilege to keep them in control and to require them to read 'in the same spirit that the author writ'. But a larger 'spirit' than Lady Byron's husband supervenes the act of writing here. The poetry, written 'in' that larger spirit, exposes that man as another partisan reader of the poem, and hence as a reader who can claim no authoritative privilege. Hobhouse's critical reading of Byron's text is written in, is part of, that larger satirical spirit. The generosity of Byron's satirical project is that it has licensed his work to bite the hand that feeds it.

III

To the degree that *Don Juan* is committed to telling the truth, the undermining of the narrator's authority has important implications.

[10] *Byron's Letters and Journals*, ed. Leslie A. Marchand (London, 1973–82), v. 93 (hereafter cited in the text as *BLJ*).

In laying 'Byron' open to criticism, the writing takes away a fundamental Romantic truth-function. Sincerity, the integrity of the
'veracious self', will not survive the poem's own processes. The
poem responds to this situation by developing a new theory of truth,
the idea of 'truth in masquerade':

> And after all, what is a lie? 'Tis but
>   The truth in masquerade; and I defy
> Historians, heroes, lawyers, priests to put
>   A fact without some leaven of a lie.
> The very shadow of true Truth would shut
>   Up annals, revelations, poesy,
> And prophecy . . .

This being the case, Byron concludes:

> Praised be all liars and all lies!

> (XI, sts. 37–8)

The project of *Don Juan* is itself an instance of the truth in masquerade:
for while six volumes of the work were published under Byron's
authority, they were all issued anonymously. Note or text, the name
Byron never passes the lips of the poem. That Byron was the author
of the work everyone knew, nor did he try to conceal the fact; but he
did equivocate, as we see very clearly in the 'Reply' he wrote (but
never published) to the attack made on *Don Juan* in *Blackwood's
Edinburgh Magazine* of August 1819.

> With regard to *Don Juan*, I neither deny nor admit it to be mine—everybody
> may form their own opinion; but, if there be any who now, or in the progress
> of that poem, if it is to be continued, feel, or should feel themselves so
> aggrieved as to require a more explicit answer, privately and personally,
> they shall have it.
>   I have never shrunk from the responsibility of what I have
> written.[11]

Byron here insists on maintaining the fiction of the author's anonym-
ity even as he all but acknowledges the poem as his production.
Not to come forward explicitly as the author of *Don Juan* meant that
the work could operate as a masquerade performance whose many
roles and attitudes would all have to be understood to have been
assumed by one person. Furthermore, the work is properly to be

[11] The text here is from *Lord Byron: Letters and Journals*, ed. Rowland E. Prothero
(London, 1898–1901), iv. 475.

designated a masquerade rather than a theatrical performance because the encounters with the poem's audiences do not take place across the distance marked by a proscenium. The poem engages its interlocutors—even when those people are a group or a class—in much more intimate and personal ways. The style is, as the work says, 'conversational'.

Still, the truth that lies in masquerade (the reader must forgive that irresistible pun) remains contradictory. In his enthusiasm for his new theory of truth the narrator exclaims 'Praised be all liars and all lies!' But the propositions concealed in that sentence—that all liars and lies are worthy of praise, and that the speaker of the sentence assents to this idea—are both belied by *Don Juan*. The text is happy to praise many lies and liars, even the lies of lying women which the younger Byron, drowning in his sentimental sexism, once had so much trouble with; and the narrator stands behind the text in all those instances. But one liar stands outside the pale: 'shuffling Southey, that incarnate lie' (x, st. 13).

The exception is extremely important so far as *Don Juan* is concerned. I pass without comment the obvious fact that Southey's exceptional position gives the lie to—contradicts—the universal praise of liars. This is important, but not so important as another contradiction. To the degree that Byron can perceive untruth incarnate in Robert Southey, to that extent Byron comes forward in his masquerade as one possessed, however unselfconsciously, of truth. A kind of negative ground of truth, Southey becomes one of the still points in the turning world of *Don Juan*. The veracity of the Byronic self is defined through its differences from and with Robert Southey.

But even here we encounter a problem, as one may see very easily from that passage in Canto III which centres on the ballad 'The isles of Greece'. At the plot level, the ballad is sung by the Romantic poet kept by Lambro on his island fastness. The song leads *Don Juan* to a series of digressive reflections on poets like Southey who sell themselves to authority, or fashion their work to catch the main chance. The textual difficulty arises because, in developing the attack on Southey's crassness and lack of integrity, the poem uses details and illustrations which are drawn from Byron's own work and career. As I have given the details of this situation elsewhere,[12] I

---

[12] See 'The Book of Byron and the Book of the World', in Jerome J. McGann, *The Beauty of Inflections: Literary Investigations in Historical Method and Theory* (Oxford, 1985), 255–93.

shall simply here underscore the general point: to wit, that in drawing
the portrait of the 'sad trimmer' poet (III, st. 82) in the likeness of
Robert Southey, Byron's poem creates an unusual palimpsest in
which the faces of Southey and Byron, those arch-antagonists, are
superimposed on each other. The two men are, in the full meaning of
that paradoxical phrase, 'Twin opposites'.

When truth operates in masquerade, then, even negative grounds
of truth fail to keep their identity. If bad 'moralists like Southey' (III,
st. 93) are not the reeds on which the poem can lean, perhaps—as
numerous readers have suggested—we are to count on the play of
Don Juan's ironies. Integrity and stability lie in the work's flaunting
of its own contradictions, in the romantic irony we observed playing
through the passage about Byron's 'veracious self' in Canto xv.
There Romantic irony is invoked, as so often in the poem, to expose
and transcend its own contradictions.

But Romantic irony is not the work's ground of truth either. We
glimpse this even through the example of Southey, who is not known
in *Don Juan* through plays of Romantic irony. He is known rather
through hatred—the same way that Brougham and Castlereagh are
known. The poem's equation of Byron and Southey, therefore, cannot be assimilated into *Don Juan*'s ironical self-understanding, for it
is an equation which, though real, stands outside—in true contradiction to—the horizon of the work's self-consciousness. Byron can
be witty at his own expense, or at Southey's expense, but his wit is
not engaged in face of the Byron/Southey parallel. His wit cannot be
engaged here because Southey is not in the end a figure of fun for
Byron, he is a figure of all that is hateful and despicable.

The issue of Southey and the presence of anger and hatred in *Don
Juan* are merely the touchstones by which we can measure the
poem's contradictions. The argument in the margins between Byron
and Hobhouse, noted earlier, eventually spills, like so much else,
into the public text:

> And recollect th[is] work is only fiction,
> And that I sing of neither mine nor me,
>   Though every scribe, in some slight turn of diction,
> Will hint allusions never *meant*. Ne'er doubt
> *This*—when I speak, I *don't hint*, but *speak out*.
>
> (xi, st. 88)

which is all very well except that the poem not only practises

such an art of allusions, it even declares itself committed to the
mode:

> '*Haud ignara loquor:*' these are *Nugae*, '*quarum*
>   *Pars* parva *fui*,' . . . but still Art and part. . . .
> '*Vertabo Cereris sacrum qui vulgaret*'—
> Which means that vulgar people must not share it.
>
> And therefore what I throw off is ideal—
>   Lower'd, leaven'd, like a history of Freemasons; . . .
> The grand Arcanum's not for men to see all;
>   My music has some mystic diapasons;
> And there is much which could not be appreciated
> In any manner by the uninitiated.

(XIV, sts. 21–2)

It is important to see that these two passages do not cancel each
other out. In *Don Juan* there is a sense in which—or perhaps it would
be better to say that there are times when—both assertions apply;
just as there are occasions when each of these attitudes would have
itself belied by the text.

Thus *Don Juan* does something more than set in motion Byron's
version of Kierkegaard's either/or problematic. The poem's contradictions, as we have seen, deconstruct all truth-functions which are
founded either in (metaphysical) Identity or (psychological) Integrity. In their place is set a truth-function founded (negatively) in
contradiction itself, and (positively) in metonymy: to the negative
either/or dialectic *Don Juan* adds the procedural rule of 'both/and'.
That procedural rule is Byron's version of what Hegel called 'the
negation of the negation'.

The latter, in its Byronic form, means that the terms of all contradictions are neither idealistically transcended nor nihilistically cancelled out. They simply remain in contradiction. The both/and rule
means that the writing of the poem must 'invariably' produce not
simply the dialectic of 'Opinions two', but somewhere 'a third too
in a nook', that third being, minimally, the awareness of the un-
resolved character of the original opposition.

It is through its many forms of contradiction that the poem
declares its truth-function to consist in the setting of problems and
not the presentation of solutions. The work is by turns playful and
rancorous, blind and perceptive. What the text says in the fragmentary Canto XVII of Juan's virtue—'I leave the thing a problem,

like all things' (st. 13)—might have been *Don Juan*'s epigraph. The point of the work is to test the limits of what it itself is able to imagine, and to carry out those tests by setting imagination against imagination.

The poem, we should therefore say, learns from itself, even though the knowledge it acquires must remain provisional, subject to change, and even sometimes unassimilated at the authoritative level of its consciousness. Byron's private argument with Hobhouse in the margins of the proofs of Cantos I–II would eventually find itself publicly displayed in the contradictory passages set down in Cantos XI and XIV, where those two imaginations expose their respective limits. This kind of thing happens repeatedly in the work. The writing seems bound to imagine the truths in its own lies as well as the falsehoods in its own truths. In *Don Juan*, Byron's imagination of Southey has a fatal appointment to keep with his imagination of himself.

This structure of provocations does not arise, however, from the ideology of Byron's own 'creative imagination'. It is rather the consequence of *Don Juan*'s rhetoric, which insists upon the presence of an objective world of various readers. One of these readers is the person we call Lord Byron, the writer of *Don Juan*, though even in *his* case, as we have seen, the person subsists in a multiplied if not even a fractured identity. But it is the many other readers—Hobhouse, Lady Byron, the reviewers—who stand as the work's most plain figures of otherness and objectivity. 'Prepare for rhyme', *Don Juan* in effect says to them all—and in so saying the work lays itself open to the preparedness—the self-consciousness—it insists upon in those it has summoned.

Don Juan is seriously interested in what they all have to say—the foolish things of William Roberts, the more thoughtful things of his friend Hobhouse, the critical and antagonistic things of everyone. In Canto VII, for example, when Byron protests against those who attacked him for underrating and scoffing 'At human power and virtue, and all that', Byron defends the morality of the work and even responds with an aggressive attack upon his attackers.

> Dogs, or Men! (for I flatter you in saying
>   That ye are dogs—your betters far) ye may
> Read, or read not, what I am now essaying
>   To show ye what ye are in every way.
>
> (VII, st. 7)

What the poem is 'now essaying', in fact, is the Siege of Ismail, which will be one of *Don Juan*'s indices for what 'human power and virtue' amount to in the brutal contemporary world. As Byron insisted in one of his letters to Murray (25 Dec. 1822), *Don Juan* was meant 'as a *satire* on the *abuses* of the present *states* of Society' (*BLJ* x. 68), and on the illusions of those who were unable to see those abuses.

But the reviewers and pamphleteers insisted that *Don Juan* was something far different. Jeffrey's notice in the *Edinburgh Review* (Feb. 1822), while respectful of the work in certain ways, summarizes the negative line of attack. *Don Juan* is 'in the highest degree pernicious' to society because it, like all Byron's writings, has 'a tendency to destroy all belief in the reality of virtue':

> *This* is the charge which we bring against Lord Byron. We say that, under some strange misapprehension as to the truth, and the duty of proclaiming it, he has exerted all the powers of his powerful mind to convince his readers, both directly and indirectly, that all ennobling pursuits and disinterested virtues, are mere deceits or illusions. . . . Love, patriotism, valour, devotion, constancy, ambition—all. . . .   (Rutherford, 201–2.)

Don Juan dissents vigorously, and effectively, from such a judgement; in the end, however, it also assimilates the judgement to itself, adds its own assent to that judgement even as it maintains, at the same time, its dissenting line.

Byron's both/and manœuvre is unmistakable, for example, at the beginning of Canto XIII. In Canto XII Byron had reiterated his position that *Don Juan*'s goal is the 'improvement' (st. 40), of society: 'My Muse by exhortation means to mend|All people' (st. 39). But at the opening of Canto XIII this passion for virtuous improvement, it appears, has waned somewhat:

> I should be very willing to redress
>   Men's wrongs, and rather check than punish crimes,
> Had not Cervantes in that too true tale
> Of Quixote, shown how all such efforts fail.   (st. 8)

Through four more stanzas Byron meditates on the 'great' if also 'sad' 'moral taught|By that real Epic' of Cervantes. It is the tale of one whose 'virtue makes him mad':

> Alas! Must noblest views, like an old song,
>   Be for mere Fancy's sport a theme creative?

That very question is one which all the negative reviews and pamphlets had themselves put to Byron's work. *Don Juan* does not answer the question here. Instead, it assumes to itself the attitude figured in the question and sets down an imagination of its truth:

> Cervantes smiled Spain's Chivalry away;
>   A single laugh demolished the right arm
> Of his own country;—seldom since that day
>   Has Spain had heroes. While Romance could charm,
> The world gave ground before her bright array;
>   And therefore have his volumes done such harm,
> That all their glory, as a composition,
> Was dearly purchased by his land's perdition.   (st. 11)

The argument repeats the most commonplace line of attack taken towards *Don Juan* by contemporary readers. Its force here as a self-critical move is only emphasized by the explicit parallels which *Don Juan* draws at various points between itself and *Don Quixote*. Furthermore, since Byron has been deliberately pursuing this (partly quixotic) line at least since the first cantos of *Childe Harold*,[13] the repetition of it here underscores the 'truth' of the idea which Jeffrey had formulated for so many: that all Byron's writings, and not just *Don Juan*, tend to undermine 'the reality of virtue'.

Byron's work is so replete with turn-abouts of this kind that we tend to read its basic structure as dialectical, and hence to approach its truth-functions in an epistemological frame of reference. This is to see the work as fundamentally critical—the great pronunciamento of what Carlyle would call the 'Everlasting Nay'. But the critical spirit that drives Byron's work is inadequately represented as a dialectical form. True, the work itself frequently encourages such a representation:

> And if I laugh at any mortal thing,
>   'Tis that I may not weep; and if I weep,
> 'Tis that our nature cannot always bring
>   Itself to apathy, for we must steep
> Our hearts first in the depths of Lethe's spring
>   Ere what we least wish to behold will sleep:
>
>   (IV, st. 4)

The passage begins with a dialectical gesture as the first two lines

---

[13] See especially Byron's Preface to Cantos I–II, where he ridicules the romanticism of the chivalric order.

put us on the brink of a neatly turned antithesis. With the third line, however, we veer off unexpectedly—not in the direction of the laughter initially imagined but toward 'apathy' and forgetfulness. These, it turns out, are neither wanted nor attainable here, though they are raised up as imaginable goals. In the end the passage does not tell us what would follow if the text were to 'weep' instead of laugh. Forgetfulness, indifference, and laughter would, by the logic of this argument, all be equally possible.

This famous passage displays in miniature an important point: that in Byron's writing, contradiction is not dialectic, it is asymmetry. Metaphoric transfers yield to the transactions of metonymy, which themselves branch out along rhizomatic lines. The order of things in the work therefore turns out to be wholly incommensurate:

> Ah!—What should follow slips from my reflection:
>   Whatever follows ne'ertheless may be
> As apropros of hope or retrospection,
>   As though the lurking thought had followed free.
>
> (xv, st. 1)

Writing 'what's uppermost, without delay' (xiv, st. 7) may equally mean description, narration, direct address; it may mean writing spontaneously or reflectively; it may mean gathering similes in a heap, developing an argument, opening a digression. It might mean copying out something (a quotation, a pharmaceutical prescription) or it might mean not writing anything at all, but simply editing.

The 'ever varying rhyme' (vii, st. 2) of *Don Juan* seems to me a direct function of its choice of a rhetorical rather than a lyrical procedure. The decision has pitched the work outside the bounds of its subjectivity and forced it to take up many matters which it may have imagined but which it could not comprehend. As a result, the writing will not—indeed, cannot—achieve anything but provisional and limited control over its own materials. It continually enters into contradictions, but the contradictions do not typically emerge out of a structure of their own internal logic. Rather, contradictions come to the work at odd angles—for instance, through structures of the unforeseen and the haphazard:

> For ever and anon comes Indigestion,
>   (Not the most 'dainty Ariel') and perplexes
> Our soarings with another sort of question:
>
> (xi, st. 3)

What undermines authority in *Don Juan* is the presence of many competing authorities, all of whom have been called to judgement. Some of these authorities are not human beings at all but circumstantial powers: Indigestion, for example, or puberty (or age), boredom, or different kinds of chance events (like the assassination of the military commandant of Ravenna, Luigi dal Pinto).[14] If all are summoned to judgement, all are equally capable of introducing unauthorized topics and problems—surprises for or threats to the text which have to be taken into account. The poem may then consciously engage with these materials or not, and when it does its engagements will themselves be highly idiosyncratic.

Don Juan develops its masquerade by pretending to be equal to itself and to all its heterodox elements. This pretence of understanding and truth is carried out, however, in the contradictory understanding that it *is* a pretence; and the ground of that contradictory understanding is the presence of others who are to observe and respond to the pretences being made.

That differential of a real otherness is most clearly to be seen in the texts that resist incorporation by Romantic irony. Because Byron's masquerade is not all in fun, for example—because many persons have been invited who are each other's mortal enemies—*Don Juan*'s pretences are not all embraceable in a comic generosity. Benevolence may be universal, but it is not everything. Savagery and tastelessness are therefore *Don Juan*'s surest signs of a collapse of its integrity, a rupture in its pretensions to the truth. Did Byron's poem imagine or anticipate the public outcry that would be raised at the passage which sneered at Southey's and Coleridge's wives as 'milliners of Bath' (III, st. 93)? Was it equal to that outrage and to the meaning which the outrage represented? We should have to say that it *was* only if we also said that, in this passage, meaning deploys itself as an unreconciled differential.

At the end of Canto XIV, as the narrator teases us about the possible outcome of Adeline's and Juan's relationship, he forecasts the actual event which will prove crucial to their lives in the plot of the poem.

> But great things spring from little:—Would you think,
> That in our youth as dangerous a passion

[14] See V, sts. 33–9.

> As e'er brought man and woman to the brink
>   Of ruin, rose from such a slight occasion,
> As few would ever dream could form the link
>   Of such a sentimental situation?
> You'll never guess, I'll bet you millions, milliards—
> It all sprung from a harmless game of billiards.

(XIV, st. 100)

A superb masquerade of truth, the passage is not at all what it may appear: for concealed in its reference to a 'harmless game of billiards' involving Juan and Lady Adeline is a private recollection of just such a game once played in 1813 by Lady Frances Wedderburn Webster and Byron.[15] But of course it was not a game of billiards at all, it was a game of hearts. In his wonderful description of the scene at the time, to Lady Melbourne, Byron observed that

> we went on with our game (of billiards) without *counting* the *hazards*—& supposed that—as mine certainly were not—the thoughts of the other party also were not exactly occupied by what was our ostensible pursuit. (*BLJ* iii. 134.)

Lady Frances and Lord Byron played out the truth of what was happening in a masquerade. They were making love, not playing billiards, but the larger truth—as Byron's letters at the time show— was that the love-making was itself masked in a series of sentimental moves and gestures.

Don Juan pretends it is forecasting the lives of its fictional characters, but while its mind is on that game of billiards, it is on something else as well, a different game of billiards which was, like the other game, not simply (or 'harmlessly') a game of billiards at all. The text here, in other words, executes a complex set of pretences as a figure for the kind of truth which poetry involves.

That truth is best seen, perhaps, in the stanza which immediately follows the one I have quoted—the stanza carrying an authoritative 'interpretation' of, or set of ethical reflections on, the 'truth' revealed in the first stanza.

> 'Tis strange—but true; for Truth is always strange,
>   Stranger than Fiction; if it could be told,
> How much would novels gain by the exchange!
>   How differently the world would men behold!

[15] For details see Leslie A. Marchand, *Byron: A Biography* (New York, 1957), i. 413–18.

How oft would vice and virtue places change!
　The new world would be nothing to the old,
If some Columbus of the moral seas
Would show mankind their souls' Antipodes.

Once the mask of truth is exposed in the first stanza, we understand how the thematized discussion in the second is equally a mask of truth. This happens because the text has revealed itself as a dialogical event in which various parties may be imagined to be participating. We may imagine, for instance, Lady Frances reading this, or Lady Melbourne, or any number of Byron's 'knowing' friends—or, for that matter, other readers, people who are unaware of the subtext. Each would have a different way of reading the passage. Furthermore, in each of those cases the authoritative interlocutor, let us call him 'Byron', would undergo an identity-shift, for the masque of truth would have to play itself out differently in each of the exchanges.

When truth comes in masquerade, propositions and states of affairs are called into question, are called to an accounting; and this includes the propositions and states of affairs which the poetical work itself appears to aver or define. Thus we might say of the poem, after Sidney, that it affirms and denies nothing—that it is, in our contemporary terms, a 'virtual' reality. That idea is often represented in *Don Juan*, as when the poem insists that it denies, admits, rejects, and contemns 'nothing'. But 'in fact' the work denies, admits, rejects, and contemns various things, though sometimes—as in the text I am alluding to—it 'in fact' denies, admits, rejects, and contemns 'nothing'. *Don Juan* is not a virtual reality, it is a particular deed in language—in*deed*, a series of particular deeds.

What is 'true' in the poem, therefore, always depends on context and circumstances. The concept of truth itself is revealed as open to change. What does not change, I think, is the structure in which knowledge and truth are pursued and (however provisionally or idiosyncratically) defined. This structure is rhetorical and dialogical—not an internal colloquy but a communicative exchange.

Finally, that structure is to be seen as a masquerade for two important reasons: that the parties to the exchange may be concretely defined, and that they may share each other's consciousness. The both/and form of the masquerade establishes the possibility of identity precisely by putting identity in question. In the same way, the pretence involved in the masquerade, being kept in the foreground, sets in motion an exchange of awarenesses from both sides of the encounter.

This is perhaps to put it all far too abstractly, so I close by suggesting that we imagine the billiard passage being read by different parties, and that we measure the differentials of truth which would emerge through those readings. Having imagined it being read (say in 1823, the year the text was published) by Lady Frances, then we might imagine Lady Frances's husband, Byron's friend Wedderburn Webster, coming to the passage ten years after that billiards game at Aston Hall, which, at the time, Webster knew nothing about. If we make the latter imagining, we might recall—would Webster have recalled it?—that on the very evening of the perilous billiards game Webster, in company with his wife and his other guests, loudly proposed a bet to Byron ' "that *he* [Webster] for a certain sum wins any given *woman*—against any given *homme* including *all friends* present["]' (*BLJ* iii. 136); and we might recall as well (would Webster have had the moral strength to make such a recollection?) that Byron 'declined' the challenge with, as Byron put it, 'becoming deference to him & the rest of the company'. What *truth* Webster's reading would have involved—*however* he read the passage!

The point is that Webster's reading, though we do not have it or even know if it was made, is part of this work's imaginings—and *that* is an important truth about *Don Juan*, and about Byron's writing in general.

CHAPTER 3

Dante Gabriel Rossetti,
or The Truth Betrayed

The transition from signs which dissimulate something to signs which
dissimulate that there is nothing, marks a decisive turning point. The
first implies a theology of truth and secrecy. . . . The second
inaugurates an age of simulacra and stimulation, in which there is no
longer . . . any last judgement to separate true from false, the real from
its artificial resurrection, since everything is already dead and risen in
advance.

JEAN BAUDRILLARD, 'The Precession of Simulacra'

BY consciously invoking his audiences in his work, Byron transformed the poetry of sincerity into a rhetorical situation. This manœuvre, in a Romantic context, allowed Byron's poetry to preserve its
Romanticism—its sincerity—as a feature of its style rather than as
an emblem of authority or morality. As a result, the whole truth
about the self (if not about the world) was laid open to a theoretical
inspection.

Consequently, Byron's work from *Manfred* onwards defines and
agrees to accept its limits. As Byron puts it in that exquisite couplet
from *Don Juan*: 'I | Have spent my life, both interest and principal, |
And deem not, what I deem'd, my soul invincible' (1 st. 213). The
wit of those punning lines, of course, testifies to the ultimate self-
confidence which is expressed in such a text. The Byronic *figura* in
Don Juan, however mortal, is never anything but wholly equal to the
competing forces and figures which his work calls out.

This confidence stems, I think, from the sense of class that is
everywhere apparent in Byron's work. Byron knows that, from a
historical perspective, his class is in process of supersession. But his
work sees the transfer of power abstractly—Romantically—as an
event that will be a long time playing itself out. Though quite
conscious of both, Byron's verse is not troubled by either social
position or money.

To the degree that his work does not come to grips with the power
of those two forces—social status and money—to that extent Byron's

work succeeds at a relatively discounted rate (or so it will seem to us). Byron *was* fortunate in his birth. Though Dante Gabriel Rossetti was not so lucky, his *work* benefited from his less favoured social circumstances. The critique of Romantic sincerity executed in Byron's work undergoes an important variation in Rossetti, who exposes the terms—they can be frightening to contemplate—within which poetry would have to find its way in the post-Byronic world, in the period Benjamin would later call 'the age of mechanical reproduction'.

I

Rossetti has a notebook entry dating from the early 1870s in which he speaks of certain 'Days when the characters of men came out as strongly as secret writing exposed to fire.'[1] What is illuminating and complex in this figure centres on the pun on the word 'characters', where both people and writing are imagined as encrypted forms— indeed, as encrypted *transforms* of each other. Their respective truths appear only when the false innocence of the surface is removed.

Rossetti's interest in 'secret writing' has little in common with those multiply coded texts we saw in *Don Juan*. Rather as with Blake when he spoke of a similar process in *The Marriage of Heaven and Hell*, the agent of revelation here is fire, and a fire associated, as in Blake, with hell. But in Blake there is nothing sinister in such fire, which is seen as a 'divine' agency (that is to say, as part of the human process of engraving). In Rossetti, however, the fire threatens because the 'characters' are sinister and threatening. Lurking below Rossetti's metaphor are suggestions of torture and even damnation, of a world in which 'the characters of men' practise concealment and deceit.

This is not an image which Rossetti would have produced when he began to test his imaginative resources in the 1840s. But it has arrived at the heart of his work, and it can help to guide us should we choose to approach him from more customary angles—for example, down the avenues of that early tale 'Hand and Soul'. This too can be a very useful point of departure, and most useful if one keeps in mind how deceptive that story is, how false its appearances.

---

[1] This is from one of the notebooks in the British Library (Ashley 1410; Notebook I, fo. 4ʳ), much of whose material remains unpublished, though W. M. Rossetti reproduced large portions of it in his 1911 edition of his brother's works; see below, n. 4.

It is a story about art, clearly, but we shall find, I think, that it has far more to say on that subject than Rossetti was aware of, at least in 1850.

Equally clearly, it has a number of things to say about love, though in fact Rossetti knew very little about that subject when he wrote 'Hand and Soul'; and what he came to learn about it later—a kind of negative knowledge, as we shall see—was not what, as an epigone of Dante, he had been expecting: not 'la salute di Beatrice', and least of all the plenitude of a divine vision, but the vacuity of his descended imagination.[2] To read Rossetti is to discover that he knew, and would come to know, very little about love itself, though he knew—and would come to know a great deal more—about the absence of love, its many forms of emptiness, its conditions of (non-) being.

Rossetti's strength as a poet grows through his penetrating anatomies of the conditions of inveterate loss: not eventual loss, those Wordsworthian losses that are born(e) in sufferance, but rather the losses that rise up before one as conditions of being rather than as occurrences. His poetry is about Fate—or, more accurately, about how fates get constructed out of the actual conditions of the life we know. All these subjects are crucial to a story like 'Hand and Soul'; but they are oblique presences, not easy to see, especially if one remains within the story's own perspective of desire.

Rossetti's obliquity is such that his work—in particular a story like 'Hand and Soul'—invites criticism to follow an analogous path of indirection, though in a spirit, one hopes, more self-conscious than was common for Rossetti.[3] 'Hand and Soul' is a richer story than another of his early tales, the unfinished piece called 'St. Agnes of Intercession'. But the latter has a scene which throws into relief the matters handled so much more indirectly in 'Hand and Soul' and in most of his finest work. This passage allegorizes, with material drawn from contemporary British life, why and how that life has been

---

[2] That imaginative descent has been most clearly traced, as an actual process, in David Riede's excellent *Dante Gabriel Rossetti and the Limits of Victorian Vision* (Ithaca, NY, 1983).

[3] The issue of Rossetti's self-consciousness is complex. In one sense, Joan Rees is clearly right when she says: 'Rossetti's inward gaze is always intense and what he sees is a drama so vivid and compelling that he must couch it in language which challenges attention by its own intensity and self-consciousness' (*The Poetry of Dante Gabriel Rossetti: Modes of Self-Expression* (Cambridge, 1981), 98). But Rossetti was not adept at 'examining his conscience', at penetrating to the structure of his brain's blindnesses and self-deceptions.

so largely erased from Rossetti's poetry. In this respect the passage may be seen to function, for Rossetti's more characteristic work, in much the same way that contemporary historical references function in Blake. The explicit referential moments in Blake's otherwise 'visionary' surfaces remind us how and why 'Rintrah' and 'Theotormon' and Blake's large networks of other mythical constructions are fundamentally creatures of the 1790s.

Like its companion tale 'Hand and Soul', 'St. Agnes of Intercession' anatomizes the character and situation of a young painter whose 'impulse towards art' was 'a vital passion' (i. 400).[4] When he falls in love with a young woman of comfortable means—as he puts it, 'of more ease than my own' (i. 402)—he is driven to seek 'such a position as would secure me from reproaching myself with any sacrifice made for her sake'. That is the young man's painfully delicate way of saying that he set about trying to become a commercially successful painter, which meant, in practical terms, submitting his work for exhibition. To this end he 'laboured constantly and unweariedly' for many days and nights on a work whose 'principal female figure' was his betrothed, Miss Mary Arden.

In these initial details we glimpse the characteristic tension which will dominate Rossetti's story: between an exalted ideal of art, on one hand, and certain quotidian practical exigencies on the other. The young man's reflections on the opening day of the exhibition make these contradictions very explicit:

My picture, I knew, had been accepted, but I was ignorant of a matter perhaps still more important,—its situation on the walls. On that now depended its success. . . . That is not the least curious feature of life as evolved in society,— . . . when a man, having endured labour, gives its fruits into the hands of other men, that they may do their work between him and mankind: confiding it to them, unknown, without seeking knowledge of them . . . without sympathy of kindred experience: submitting to them his naked soul, himself, blind and unseen . . . (i. 403.)

Centrally at issue here is the work's public and commercial 'success', as opposed to its 'artistic achievement' or 'intrinsic value'. Or rather, the passage shows how the sensibility of a man who is committed to the 'intrinsic values' of art suffers a crucifixion of the imagination when

[4] My texts for Rossetti's work will be taken from *The Collected Works of Dante Gabriel Rossetti*, 2 vols. (London, 1886). For texts not available in this edition I have used *The Works of Dante Gabriel Rossetti* (London, 1911). Both collected editions were edited by W. M. Rossetti. Where necessary, page-numbers are given in the text.

he feels compelled to operate in and through the mediations 'evolved in society'. To his initial anxiety about whether his picture will even be accepted for exhibition succeed a whole train of others which crystallize in one immediate concern: whether the painting will be prominently displayed—in the jargon of the day, whether it will be 'on the line'—or whether it will be relegated to some less prestigious, or even less visible, position.

These misgivings surface as soon as he begins to make a tour of the exhibition with another man, also unnamed in the story, whom the painter accidentally encounters. This man, a poet and an art-critic, gives a further turn of the screw to the young painter's anxieties:

> My companion's scrutiny was limited almost entirely to the 'line', but my own glance wandered furtively among the suburbs and the outskirts of the ceiling, and a misgiving possessed me that I might have a personal interest in those unenviable 'high places' of art. . . . [S]till I dared not institute an open search for my own [painting], lest thereby I should reveal to my companion its presence in some dismal condemned corner which might otherwise escape his notice. (i. 404.)

But while Rossetti's painter fears and therefore respects his com-panion's power in the culture-industry of their world, he has nothing but contempt for the artistic taste and poetic skills of this 'hippo-potamus-fronted man, with his splay limbs and wading gait' (i. 404). As the two pause in their tour of the exhibition, the critic pulls out a sheaf of his poems and asks the young painter for his opinion. After reading them hurriedly Rossetti's protagonist manages an answer. It is a nice moment:

> 'I think,' I replied coolly, 'that when a poet strikes out for himself a new path in style, he should first be quite convinced that it possesses sufficient advantages to counterbalance the contempt which the swarm of his imitators will bring upon poetry.'
> My ambiguity was successful. I could see him take the compliment to himself, and inhale it like a scent, while a slow broad smile covered his face. It was much as if, at some meeting, on a speech being made complimentary to the chairman, one of the waiters should elbow that personage aside, plant his knuckles on the table, and proceed to return thanks. (i. 407.)

A great deal could be said about this passage. So far as Rossetti's young painter is concerned, it dramatizes the deep connections joining his artistic fastidiousness and 'idealism' to his tortured duplicity and servile cowardice. 'Successful' is just the right word, in this context, to describe his wary but contemptuous reply to the other man's fatuous request for praise. If he wants to be 'successful' as an artist, this critic may be a man to cultivate. So the young painter stays with him throughout the exhibition, suffering the man's absurd self-importance. On the other hand, if he wants to be true to his own sense of himself, he cannot lie about the man's bad verse. So he equivocates and thereby saves the situation 'on both sides'. But one can equally see how this situation has thereby also been 'lost on both sides', for the painter has not behaved honestly—indeed, has compromised his own expressed 'ideals' in order not to offend a person who might possibly help advance his artistic 'success'.

Other compromises are also at work. So far as Rossetti is concerned, the message is a darker version of that famous moment in Joyce's *Portrait of the Artist as a Young Man*, when we are given Stephen's (distinctly Pre-Raphaelite) poem 'Are you not weary of ardent ways'. Joyce, of course, mocks his *alter ego* Stephen Dedalus, whose 'poem' is meant to be seen as derivative, and thus doubly decadent. In a similar way, when Rossetti's supplies an example of *his* character's verse, he cuts an irony which underscores the self-reflexive character of his parodistic poem.

> Like ranks in calm unipotence
>   Swayed past, compact and regular,
>   Time's purposes and portents are:
> Yet the soul sleeps, while in the sense
> The graven brows of Consequence
>   Lie sunk, as in blind wells the star.
>
> O gaze along the wind-strewn path
>   That curves distinct upon the road
>   To the dim purple-hushed abode.
> Lo! Autumntide and aftermath!
> Remember that the year has wrath
>   If the ungarnered wheat corrode.
>
>   (i. 406–7)

In 'St. Agnes of Intercession' Rossetti splits his *alter ego* into the two characters of writer and painter. When the painter of the story then exposes the fatuousness of the writer, the full structure of Rossetti's artistic hopes and fears, his pretensions and insecurities, is laid out. Both the story's Rossettian *figurae* have power, but only to undermine the authority and aspirations of the other.

The entire scene from 'St. Agnes of Intercession', written in 1848–50 (but revised in 1870),[5] is thus an emblem of Rossetti's career as an artist and poet. Later I shall return to deal with the matter of Miss Mary Arden—that is to say, with Rossetti's habit of linking his artistic ideals and imaginative practices to the women whose images dominated his life. For now I wish to concentrate on the problem of the material conditions of artistic production as Rossetti experienced them in his age. Unlike Blake's and Byron's, Rossetti's work does not foreground the artistic opportunities which are offered when an artist seeks to utilize the physical and institutional structures within which all such work is necessarily carried out. Rossetti is as self-conscious as they are about those media, but to him the structures more often rose up as obstacles to be overcome rather than adventures to be risked. 'St. Agnes of Intercession', in the scene I have been recapitulating, pays greatest attention to the difficulties raised by the institutions of imagination: most particularly, those means of production which establish the possibility, or the terms, on which a painter or a poet is able to encounter an audience.

If Rossetti's feeling for those difficulties makes him a less innocent poet than either Blake or Byron, it also set him in a position where he could explore, far more profoundly than any English poet had previously done, the significance of imaginative work in an age of mechanical reproduction, in an age where 'the best that has been known and thought in the world' is seen to be quite literally a *product*, the output of what we now call the 'culture-' or the 'consciousness-industries'. Like Baudelaire in France, Rossetti was the first poet in England to see this very clearly; and, again like Baudelaire, he recoiled from it, and tried to imagine ways for evading those institutional powers, and for recovering an ideal of artistic and poetic transcendence. But like Baudelaire once again, what he accomplished was far more important. What he accomplished was a critical exposure of the symbolistic imagination: that it is a style designed to function within a marketing and commercial frame of reference.

II

In that context, Rossetti is constantly driven to work by indirection. This happens because he operates in the belief—the ideology—that

---

[5] According to W. M. Rossetti (*Works*, i. 525–6).

life is one thing, art another. Art for Rossetti appeared to him—as in Chiaro's vision in 'Hand and Soul'—as life in its finer tone, the one certain means by which human beings can soar beyond the confusions of a mortal and veiled existence. His ideology of the sacred character of the poetic life made him an acute observer of the illusions of the quotidian world—in this he is like his sister Christina. But whereas, for her, sacramentalism—the ritually practised religious life—was the one fundamental necessity, for Dante Gabriel that necessity was located in the practise of art.

This point of view established the basic contradiction within which Rossetti's work was to develop. The practical dimension of the contradiction can be expressed as follows: how does one paint or write poetry when the world of getting and spending constantly impinges, transforming the fair illusion of a pure pursuit of Beauty into other, darker forms—at worst unworthy, at best distracting, but in any case equally illusionistic? This is the great contradiction raised by poetry in the age of Victorian commercial imperialism, and first given profound expression in Tennyson's 1832 *Poems*. Rossetti would not find a solution to that problem, any more than anyone else would. In fact the problem has no solution, because its importance as a problem lies not in any realities it consciously questions but in the illusions it unwittingly exposes. It is a problem without a solution because it is a problem framed within its own rooted misunderstanding about the nature of art and imagination: that these are transcendental forms standing free of the sublunary orders of human things.

One face of the illusion appears as the idea that 'effort and expectation and desire', or striving, seeking, and finding, will eventually produce a solution. Rossetti is the first Victorian poet to show clearly the falseness of such convictions. The important secondary illusion is that the sublunary world and the world of art differ from each other in every important respect—as the material world is thought to differ in all important respects from the world of spirit. This illusion Rossetti will also discredit, at first with excitement and confidence, in his explorations of erotic experience, but finally in fear and trembling, as the full import of his erotic explorations slowly dawns upon him. In the end Rossetti's poetry (and his art as well, though I shall not be concentrating on that aspect of his work)[6]

[6] See Riede's book, *passim*, for an excellent handling of the parallel forms of Rossetti's imaginative work.

will recuperate Dante's journey in the opposite direction, descending from various illusory heavens through a purgatory of unveilings to the nightmares and hells of his greatest work, the unwilled revelations arrived at in *The House of Life*.

It is important to realize that Rossetti did everything in his power to cherish his illusions—and to persuade others that the world was not a vale of tears but a vale of beautiful soul-making. 'Hand and Soul' is a hoax in more ways than one. It is a hoax, formally speaking, because it consciously imitates the literary hoaxes of Edgar Allen Poe—those tales like 'Von Kempelen and his Discovery' which present themselves to the reader as non-fictions. 'Hand and Soul', written in the form of a personal essay, 'deceived more than one admirer of it who made enquiry in Florence and Dresden after the pictures of Chiaro' (ii. 524). Like Poe and Baudelaire, Rossetti catches out the hypocritical reader by feeding him interesting or charming illusions. The ultimate point of such a story is to expose the structure of those illusions.

But, unlike Poe and Baudelaire, Rossetti himself more than half believed in the illusions raised by his story. For Rossetti, then, the story is not initially conceived as a hoax at all but as a serious conjuring-trick. 'In his imaginative adventures', R. L. Megroz has acutely said, 'Rossetti was always casting the horoscope of his life'.[7] 'Hand and Soul' is in this respect, at least initially, a serious act of magic, an effort to put into writing a story that might prove to be the actual plot of his own life. If the story could be imagined to be true, in the second half of the nineteenth century in England (either as a piece of 'past' history or as the sketch of the true 'future'), then art could be said to transcend circumstance. And Rossetti was not the only one who sought to turn the fictions of that story into truths.

But the story is a hoax, both formally and in fact. Yet Rossetti insisted on believing his own fiction about the artist's mission to unveil heavenly existences. In this insistence lies the greatness, and the horror, of his life's work. For thereby he completed the curve of the demonic imagination outlined half a century before by Blake, who showed how 'he who will not defend Truth may be compelled to | Defend a Lie, that he may be snared & caught & taken' (*Milton*, 8: 47).

Chiaro's visionary maiden painted in his supreme masterpiece,

---

[7] R. L. Megroz, *Dante Gabriel Rossetti, Painter Poet of Heaven and Earth* (London, 1928), 185.

and the Mary Arden who sat for the young painter in 'St. Agnes of Intercession', are the same person seen in the different planes of their reality. They are together a *figura* of Rossetti's secular rite of transubstantiation, or of his consubstantial existence. One is 'an image . . . of thine own soul within thee' (i. 392), while the other is the materialization of that soul as a historical reality. One is temporally and socially located in order to 'prove' that the other is no mere phantasm, while the other is dematerialized in order to show that material reality has a spiritual dimension (vulgarly, in Rossetti's case, that love is not simply sex).

The problem for Rossetti is that both these ideas are fictions— seizures of the imagination which might be either truth (as Keats insisted) or machines (as E. T. A. Hoffmann, and Poe, would suggest). To decide that crucial question Rossetti made an experiment of his life and his life's work, where his deepest convictions were put to a series of empirical tests. Elizabeth Siddal is, in this sense (and in this sense only), Mary Arden; and the artist who attaches himself to her, who literally draws her into his life (that is a pun to which Rossetti himself would often resort), and who finally marries and loses her, is Chiaro and the unnamed artist of 'St. Agnes of Intercession'. Rossetti's life between 1847 and 1862 is the empirical completion of those narrative imaginings.

But the true history did not turn out to be the story Rossetti wanted to tell, or that he thought he had told. In the first place, the artist's life Rossetti came to know in those years had none of the mythic purity of Chiaro's tale. Rossetti had to scramble for success, seek out commissions, constantly resupply himself with the money he loved to call 'tin' (thereby dismissing it from the serious concerns he kept imagining for himself). The more he made his way as an artist, the more difficult he found the demands that such a life placed upon him. These were not the grandiose spiritual difficulties laid upon the high-minded Chiaro; they were crass and quotidian demands, nightmarishly worse even than those glimpsed in 'St. Agnes of Intercession'.

Rossetti had various tricks by which he held off the enormity of this experimental life that he was pursuing. He paraded his refusals to exhibit in the ordinary professional ways, and he nurtured the myth, both for himself and for others, of Bohemian genius. But while Millais, Brown, and Edward Jones were making their way by more conventional means, Rossetti was none the less making his way—in

certain respects, not least of all monetary, even more successfully.
But it was a way that left only ashes in his mouth.

Nothing shows his situation so well as his relations with the
people whose commissions he was seeking. It began with the earliest
of them, Francis McCracken for instance, in the early fifties. Perceiving
McCracken as 'as absolute Guy—worse than Patmore' (L i. 185),[8]
Rossetti manipulated him into buying things at grossly inflated
prices, and then ridiculed him to his friends—for example in this
parody of Tennyson's 'The Kraken' which he called 'Maccraken':

> Getting his pictures, like his supper, cheap
>   Far far away in Belfast by the sea,
> His scaly, one-eyed, uninvaded sleep
>   Mac Cracken sleepeth. While the PRB
> Must keep the shady side, he walks a swell
>   Through spungings of perennial growth & height
>   And far away in Belfast out of sight
> By many an open do and secret sell
>   Fresh daubers he makes shift to scarify
> And fleece with pliant shears the slumbering green.
> There he has lied, though aged, and will lie,
>   Fattening on ill-got pictures in his sleep,
>   Till some Pre-Raphael prove for him too deep.
> Then once by Hunt & Ruskin to be seen,
> Insolvent he shall turn & in the Queen's Bench die.[9]

Throughout the fifties and sixties Rossetti cosseted and condescended
to his buyers. They seemed, most of them, altogether too easy
marks: eager, relatively ignorant, contemptible in the end. To Ford
Madox Ford, for example, he remarked:

I'll forebear from springing at the unaccustomed throat of Trist, if possible;
but really a man shouldn't buy pictures without nerving himself beforehand
against commercial garotte. (L ii. 520.)

This sort of thing is a refrain in his letters. Yet his own idealization
of the practice of art turned his behaviour into a kind of self-
immolation. If Trist and the other buyers were suffering executions

---

[8] References to Rossetti's letters are from *Letters of Dante Gabriel Rossetti*, ed. Oswald
Doughty and John Robert Wahl, 4 vols. (Oxford, 1965), cited in the text as *L* followed
by volume- and page-number.
[9] The text here is taken from Rossetti's MS letter to Allingham in the Morgan
Library; see also *L* i. 164.

in their wallets, Rossetti's 'commercial garotte' was strangling his own soul.

By 1865–6 Rossetti had become a very successful painter indeed, measured in terms of both his celebrity and his income. At the same time it had become apparent, to himself in any case, that his experiment with his life and his ideals had not gone well. The course of his commercial career had its parallel in the course of his devotional life—by which I mean his love-life. Elizabeth's suicide in 1862 was no more than the exponent and capstone of his disastrous quests for the Beatrice which his experiment required. Their life together had not been an 'ideal' in any sense, either before or after the marriage, though his initial imagination of her meaning for him was—just that, that she was to be deeply meaningful. Then too were his infidelities, we do not know exactly how many. In a sense they were not infidelities to Elizabeth at all, since his attachment to her was never personal. What he worshipped was her image, and that he had himself created, first in his imagination, and then later, in the series of incredible drawings and paintings which he devoted to that image. His were infidelities, therefore, to his own soul, to his idea of himself, to the vision which had come to Chiaro in the late 1840s.

The extent of those infidelities were defined for him in the death of his wife and unborn child. The most celebrated act of his life— burying his volume of largely unpublished poems in the coffin with Elizabeth—was a form of expiation, of course, but its full significance has to be understood in the context of his artistic and poetic careers. His steady success as a painter became for Rossetti an index of how he was betraying his mission as an artist. The greater his success in securing commissions, the more erratic his output as a painter became. His cynical attitude toward his various patrons was matched only by his scandalous failure to meet obligations even after he had been paid. Through it all, however, he began to imagine that what he was betraying as a painter he was preserving as a poet. His paintings were hopelessly entangled with commercial affairs, but his poetry, it seemed to him, had been nurtured apart from worldly concerns. When in the autumn of 1860 he sent a manuscript book of his original poetry to William Allingham for comments and criticism, his accompanying remarks are revealing:

When I think how old most of these things are, it seems like a sort of mania to keep thinking of them still, but I suppose one's leaning still to them depends mainly on their having no trade associations, and being still a sort of thing of one's own. I have no definite ideas as to doing anything with them, but should like, even if they lie at rest, to make them as good as I can. (*L.* i. 377.)

After he published, successfully, *The Early Italian Poets* in 1861, a volume of his original work was advertised, *Dante at Verona and Other Poems.* But Elizabeth's death intervened, along with the accompanying sense that his unfaithfulness was not simply, or even fundamentally, marital. The gift of his book of poems to Elizabeth's corpse was a gesture asserting that his artistic soul was still alive, and that he still had the integrity to preserve its life. He sent his poems out of the world.

But this left him more painfully in the world than ever, and the years 1862–8 are a record of what Oswald Doughty once labelled 'Disillusion' and 'Success'.[10] For Rossetti these were two faces of the same reality. Doughty's terms apply to Rossetti's artistic career, but they carry ironical overtones because, so far as Rossetti was concerned, his very success as a painter only multiplied his sense of moral disillusion. In this connection, though we must be very clear about the commercialism of the paintings, we are precisely *not* to judge the significance of those paintings through Rossetti's contradicted Victorian ideology. He despised the commercial face he saw in his work, but we must read and judge that work in another light.

If the paintings were commercial to a degree—and they were— they triumph in and through that commercialism. Like the poems, they are deceptions, sometimes even self-deceptions. Formally considered, they often appear to us as genre-paintings; but the appearance is deceptive, for the work he was trying to sell was largely a series of abstract experiments in the use of colour and (most importantly) the conventions of painterly space. Rossetti's composition and his use of colour have never been seriously faulted, but many have complained about his draughtsmanship. It is the drawing, however, which most graphically reveals the experimental character of his work, for it is the drawing which tilts his pictures out of their conventional structures. These paintings seduce and then abandon the corrupted eye of the conventional viewer, and in the process they contrive to deliver a secret meaning through the surface of betrayed appearances.

[10] These are the titles of chs. 1 and 2 in Book iii of his biography *A Victorian Romantic: Dante Gabriel Rossetti* (London, 1949).

In this way Rossetti experiences an overthrow of certain traditional ideas about success and failure in art, illusion and disillusion in life. His success and disillusion are both real. But in his work we observe success being measured by disillusion, and disillusion being founded on success.

This pattern is recurrent and clearly displayed in the case of his poetical work as well. In 1868–9, finding it impossible to paint at all, he began writing poetry again. After much urging by relatives and friends, he published sixteen of these new sonnets in the *Fortnightly Review* (March 1869), and in the succeeding months he continued to write. Eventually he began to articulate the possibility of exhuming the book he had buried with Elizabeth, as part of a project to print (but not to publish)

some old and new poems—chiefly old—for private circulation. . . . My object is to keep them by me as stock to be added to for a possible future volume; but in any case I thought it necessary to print them, as I found blundered transcripts of some of my old things were flying about, and would some time have got into print perhaps,—a thing afflictive to one's bogie. (*L* ii. 716–17.)

Rossetti's tentative moves toward returning his poetry to the world were given a crucial impetus when he read an anonymous article on his verse in *Tinsley's Magazine* in August 1869, at the very time he was working on the proofs for his 'Trial Book' of poems. Once again he clearly describes the dialectic which is driving his new writing:

so after twenty years one stranger does seem to have discovered one's existence. However I have no cause to complain, since I have all I need of an essential kind, and have taken little trouble about it,—except always in the nature of my work,—the poetry especially in which I have done no potboiling at any rate. So I am grateful to that art, and nourish against the other that base grudge which we bear those whom we have treated shabbily. (*L* ii. 729.)

It is an astonishing passage for a man who, in 1869, had the kind of celebrity and success which Rossetti enjoyed. That H. Buxton Forman—the young author of the *Tinsley's* piece—should write an essay on Rossetti's poetry, when so little had appeared in print, and most of that in relatively inaccessible places, testifies to the kind of attention which his name commanded. Yet to Rossetti it seemed that his very existence had only just then been discovered, after twenty years of—what, invisibility? Yes, this was the way he saw it:

the blankness which his commercial work as a painter had left where the image of his soul had once appeared.

III

Late in 1869, therefore, Rossetti began putting together a book of poetry which was to recoup those losses and betrayals he had been accumulating since the early fifties. He was full of anxiety about every detail of this project. Between mid-August 1869 and 1 March 1870 he received for correction and revision at least three sets of initial proofs (20 Aug.–21 Sept.), two so-called Trial Books (3 Oct.– 25 Nov.), and a final complete proof of the first edition. The changes made in these proofs and Trial Books were massive: many poems were added and some were removed; large additions were written into the proof-materials at all six major stages; titles were changed, and numerous local corrections and alterations were made; and finally, not least significant, the ordering of the poems underwent important and radical transformations. In the next two months, April and May, Rossetti continued to harass his publishers with extensive revisions and large-scale alterations of every kind. Nor was the physical appearance of the book a matter of small moment: the paper, the binding, the cloth, the colour, the kind of dies to be struck for the embossed cover designs, and so forth—all these matters engrossed his attention. Rossetti's *Poems* of 1870 were bringing the whole soul of the man into activity.[11]

To Rossetti's imagination, that soul was the one he had almost lost through his life of betrayal—through his worldliness. But in objective truth it was another, more demonic soul to which his life's work had been devoted, and entirely faithful. Rossetti's concern that his book make a good appearance, in every sense, reflects his desire that it be a perfect image of beauty, of finishedness, of his commitment to perfection. His notorious efforts to control as completely as possible the immediate critical reception of the book must be understood as part of his obsession with the appearance of his work, the impression it would create. By 1870 he had a large network of

[11] The best account of the Trial Books and the publication history of the 1870 volume is Janet Camp Troxell's 'The "Trial Books" of Dante Gabriel Rossetti', repr. from *The Colophon*, NS 3/2 (1938) in *The Princeton University Library Chronicle*, 33 (1972), 177–92; but see also Robert N. Keane, 'D. G. Rossetti's *Poems*, 1870: A Study in Craftsmanship', ibid. 193–209.

friends and friendly acquaintances who were well connected in the periodical press. All were enlisted to launch the book into the world—in pre-publication reviews wherever possible—not simply to a chorus of praise, but in terms that were to represent Rossetti's *Poems* as a work of the greatest artistic moment—indeed, as the very exponent and symbol of what 'a work of art' meant.[12]

In this sense, Rossetti's *Poems* (1870)—even more than Swinburne's *Poems and Ballads* (1866), which had created such a sensation four years earlier—is a manifesto for what Pater would call 'Aesthetic Poetry'. Comprised in that event, however, as Walter Benjamin so acutely observed in his great work on Baudelaire, is the understanding that the 'work of art' has now identified itself with, and as, the commodity.[13] The work was to be so carefully prepared, so thoroughly worked and polished, so packaged and promoted that it would ravish its audience and establish Rossetti's fame. The book was meant to 'succeed' in the same way, only far more absolutely, that the painter, in 'St. Agnes of Intercession', set out to succeed. Consumed for months with his corrections and revisions, Rossetti was perhaps able to blink the commercial forms and 'trade associations' that were concealed in this attention to his craft, but the commodity-status of his work emerges very clearly in those other investments: his obsession with his book's physical appearance, on one hand, and—crucially—his campaign to manage the reviews, on the other.

But if Rossetti's *Poems* (1870) return and re-establish the contradictions he had begun to explore in the late forties and early fifties, the intervening years had made an enormous difference in his work. In those years a happy liberal view might look for, and might even discover, signs of a 'growing artistic maturity', of a 'development' towards, some 'greater self-consciousness' in his work which could suggest that he had 'transcended' in some measure the network of initial contradictions.[14] But in fact Rossetti's 'development', if one

[12] See Doughty, *A Victorian Romantic*, 439–53 for a good account of Rossetti's campaign to control the reviews.

[13] See Walter Benjamin, *Charles Baudelaire: A Lyric Poet in the Era of High Capitalism*, trans. Harry Zohn (London, 1973).

[14] In a sense, of course, Rossetti's work does make an advance from the relatively unselfconscious and even innocent work of the early years. What I mean to indicate here is the inadequacy of the commonplace idea that Rossetti's poetry, as it develops, gains some kind of wisdom or imitable moral depth. Indeed, it seems to me that the climax of his career was 'penultimate' in the sense that, after he completed the work

can call it that, is in the opposite direction—towards a more complete immersion within the contradictions, indeed, towards an enslavement to them. In twenty years Rossetti had moved from the margin to the very heart of his culture: as Blake would have said, 'he became what he beheld'. In tracing that movement, *Poems* (1870) achieved its greatness. The analogy to *Les Fleurs du mal* is quite exact, so that what Benjamin said of the latter can be applied, *pari passu*, to Rossetti:

There is little point in trying to include the position of a Baudelaire in the fabric of the most advanced position in mankind's struggle for liberation. From the outset it seems more promising to investigate his machinations where he undoubtedly is at home—in the enemy camp. Very rarely are they a blessing for the opposite side. Baudelaire was a secret agent—an agent of the secret discontent of his class with its own rule.[15]

In Rossetti's case as well, therefore, 'the point of departure is the object riddled with error' (103). And in the nineteenth century there are few English books of poetry more secretly discontented, more riddled with error, than this book of Rossetti's.

We may begin to unriddle that error by a critical retracing of the book's history. In his reply to Buchanan's 'The Fleshly School of Poetry', Rossetti defended his dramatic monologue 'Jenny' by a general argument about the nature of art. When he first wrote the poem 'some thirteen years ago', he understood that the subject-matter—a young man's visit to a prostitute—might have called for 'a treatment from without', so that the reader would be able to see the poem casting a clear critical judgement on such a scene. Such an objective treatment would have set a critical distance between the poem and its problematic subject. Rossetti rejected this procedure, however, for

the motive powers of art reverse the requirement of science, and demand first of all an *inner* standing-point. The heart of such a mystery as this must be plucked from the very world in which it beats and bleeds; and the beauty and pity . . . can come with full force only from the mouth of one alive to its whole appeal, such as the speaker put forward in the poem,—that is, of a young and thoughtful man of the world.   (ii. 484–5.)

This is more than the classic defence, that poems are not to be

for the 1870 volume and the associated *House of Life* poetry, Rossetti's verse exhibited a sharp falling-off, a collapse that parallels the curve of his last years.

[15] Benjamin, *Baudelaire*, 104 n. The quotation immediately following is from p. 103.

read as 'personal expressions'. Rossetti is rather speaking as a student of Browning, whose work with the dramatic monologue Rossetti so much admired. In that form an effort is made to confine subjectivity to the core of what Coleridge once called the 'dramatic truth of such situations, supposing them real'.[16] The dramatic monologue moves to take the 'lyrical' out of the 'ballad'. Rossetti's '*inner* standing-point' is thus a Victorian explanation of what Keats called 'negative capability', or the process by which the author's conscious separation from his subject—the typical structure of a poem by, say, Rochester or Pope—is cancelled in a process of deep sympathetic engagement. In Rossetti's case, however, as in Browning's, the chameleonic turn involves a transfer of sympathy from the poet to some figure or character who is concretely imagined in the poem. The so-called 'poetry of experience' becomes, in Victorian hands, a form for introducing modes of subjectivity into historically removed materials, or into contemporary materials which might be, for various reasons, problematic.

In the Victorian dramatic monologue, this transfer of sympathy cancels the traditional structure on which the identity of the poet, formally speaking, depends. Browning was not especially interested in, or perhaps even aware of, the crisis (and therefore the opportunity) which was emerging for poetry in this dismantling of the conventions of sincerity. But Rossetti was. Browning's spy will succeed to the absent gods of Flaubert and later Joyce, who stand apart from their creations, paring their fingernails. This is the theory, or rather the ideology, in which Rossetti too has taken his stand.

But as with Baudelaire's *flâneur*, Rossetti's disengagement becomes an exponent of social alienation, as is quite clear in 'Jenny' itself. The sympathy of Rossetti's 'young and thoughtful man of the world' is for a sleeping figure, a prostitute who never responds and who in the poem cannot respond. Her condition, however, merely replicates the incompetent thought and limited sympathies of the young man. He does not understand her, or her 'case', because she exists for him in an aesthetic condition alone, that state where sympathy appears as the indifference of appreciation. In the end, both prostitute and young man are figures of poetry's own latent structures of alienation as they have descended into Rossetti's hands. In fact, the image of that 'thoughtful' young man's soul is revealed here as self-contradicted,

---

[16] See *Biographia Literaria*, ed. James Engell and W. J. Bate (Princeton, 1983) ii. 6.

an image with the face of a prostitute superimposed on the face of his sister.

In 'Jenny', the frame erected by the dramatic monologue works to reveal alienation rather than establish sympathy, and to suggest—ultimately—that the dramatic monologue is a construction of Chinese boxes. More than recording a failed quest for sympathetic engagement, the poem judges this to be the failure of poetry (or art) itself. This judgement is an extremely crucial one, in the nineteenth century, because poetry and art were then generally regarded as the ultimate depositories, and even the creators, of spiritual and human values. In calling that ideology into question, Rossetti's work has contrived to imagine the experience of being distanced altogether from experience. It is to have fashioned a vehicle for conveying, quite literally, *the feeling of the absence of feeling.*[17]

Nowhere is this experience more clearly visible than in *The House of Life*, which must be the most alienated, and probably the most horrifying, major poem in the language. This culminant achievement is so much integrated with his whole life's work, and in particular with the project that became *Poems* (1870), that the connections have to be sketched. *Poems* (1870), we may recall, is separated into three parts. The initial section is composed principally of a series of longer pieces—dramatic monologues, stories, ballads, and a few translations. Here the deployment of Rossetti's '*inner* standing-point' is most clearly shown—not simply in monologues like 'A Last Confession' and 'Jenny', but in all the literary ballads ('Troy Town', 'Stratton Water', 'Sister Helen', and so forth), where the use of the ballad convention historicizes the style and voicing as well as the narrative materials. The point of view in 'Dante at Verona', similarly antiqued, is much closer to Dante's age than to Rossetti's. Likewise, Rossetti employs translation, here and elsewhere, as yet another depersonalizing convention. The third section of *Poems* (1870), which follows *The House of Life*, is largely devoted to a variant type of Rossettian translation: 'Sonnets for Pictures', so called.

Paradoxically, Rossetti's use of these non-subjective verse-forms intensifies the aura of poetic self-consciousness. He turns away from his own age and self, but in doing so the contemporaneous relevance of his acts of historical displacement is only heightened. 'Dante at Verona' is in this respect a clear allegory, but an allegory which

[17] Rossetti's paintings—and Burne-Jones's, for that matter—are similarly charged.

deconstructs itself. Dante's alienation has its contemporary (Rossettian) analogy in the speaker of the poem, who celebrates the critique of luxurious society which Dante executes. But whereas the Dante of Rossetti's poem speaks out openly and plainly against the world of Can Grande, there is no plain speaking at the contemporary level, merely gestures and vague allusions:

> But wherefore should we . . . be at strife
>   From the worn garment of a life
> To rip the twisted ravel out?
>   Good needs expounding; but of ill
> Each hath enough to guess his fill.

Yet in a society like Rossetti's, so luxurious and self-deceived, to attempt an exposition of 'the good' is to run in peril of mere cant, while to leave the 'ill' to guesswork and generality is to court inconsequence. Rossetti's poem is well aware of the need for the plain speaking which its Dante represents, but which it itself cannot summon. After quoting a particularly effective denunciation by Dante of the 'priests and money-changers' of Florentine society, Rossetti's poem observes:

> For ever well our singers should
> Utter good words and know them good
> Not through song only . . .

The figure of Dante is, in the end, a reproach to Rossetti and the poets of his age, a scandalous presence; and the success of Rossetti's poem lies partly in the sucess with which it dramatizes the scandal of its own analogies.

But 'Dante at Verona' does not exemplify what is best and most innovative in Rossetti's poetry. To see that, in the non-personal and antiqued material, we have to look at some other things—for example, the excellent 'An Old Song Ended', which begins by quoting the last stanza of an antique ballad and then 'ends' it with four more stanzas. The story, rendered in the convention of a dialogue between a dying lady—a Mariana figure—and an unnamed interlocutor, let us know that she will die before her lover returns. The poem finishes with the lady's last reply to the final question put to her:

> 'Can you say to me some word
> I shall say to him?'

> 'Say I'm looking in his eyes
> Though my eyes are dim.'

This is quintessential Rossetti, an ambiguous icon constructed from a play on the phrase 'looking in'. Henceforth the lady will be haunting her absent lover, in the same way that Rossetti is haunted by the old song. (That connection between lady and old song, in fact, makes the absent lover an obvious *figura* of Rossetti and the contemporary poet.) Henceforth an 'external' presence who will be looking into his eyes as he observes the external world, she becomes as well an internal ghost who, though dead, is destined to live on in the way he looks at his world.

This haunted and self-conscious figure is at the heart of all Rossetti's poems and paintings. We rightly see a poem like 'The Blessed Damozel' as typical work for just that reason. Of all the verse printed in the first section of *Poems* (1870), 'The Stream's Secret' is closest to *The House of Life*. But 'The Blessed Damozel' is more relevant for understanding the sonnet sequence because its antiqued character highlights how the '*inner* standing-point' works in those sonnets. Rossetti disjoins himself from the first-person speaker in 'The Blessed Damozel' by invoking the formalities of the ballad convention; but because he does not historicize his materials as clearly and resolutely as he does (say) in 'Stratton Water' or his other old tales, the scenes in the poem appear to float in a kind of abstraction, outside space and time. That ambiguous condition, where one feels unmoored and alienated even as one seems to live a determinate and eventual existence, defines what we know as *The House of Life*.

IV

The House of Life is more than a presentation, or case history, of personality dismemberment. It is that, of course, but it is also part of a project—an execution—of such dismemberment, an active agent in the destructive project it is unfolding. This complicity is what makes the work, and the whole volume which it epitomizes, so fearful and so magnificent. The sonnets record a history by which 'changes' associated with a period of 'Youth'—these are figured principally as the changing experiences of love—are finally transfixed in (and as) the immobilized forms of 'Fate'. The history unfolds through a set of losses and disintegrations which culminate as the loss of identity.[18]

At the outset of the sequence, the notorious sonnet 'Nuptial Sleep' appears far removed from the terrible images which emerge in the concluding six sonnets.

> At length their long kiss severed with sweet smart:
>   And as the last slow sudden drops are shed
>   From sparkling eaves when all the storm has fled,
> So singly flagged the pulses of each heart.
> Their bosoms sundered, with the opening start
>   Of married flowers to either side outspread
>   From the knit stem; yet still their mouths, burnt red,
> Fawned on each other where they lay apart.
>
> Sleep sank them lower than the tide of dreams,
>   And their dreams watched them sink, and slid away.
> Slowly their souls swam up again, through gleams
>   Of watered light and dull drowned waifs of day;
> Till from some wonder of new woods and streams
>   He woke, and wondered more: for there she lay.
>
>   (5/6a)[19]

Here is the work's supreme imagination of triumph. One might not appreciate this fact because the previous sonnet, 'The Kiss', represents an actual experience of erotic consummation. It is, moreover, an experience recorded for us in the first person:

> I was a child beneath her touch,—a man
>   When breast to breast we clung, even I and she,—
>   A spirit when her spirit looked through me,—
> A god when all our life-breath met to fan
> Our life-blood, till love's emulous ardours ran,
>   Fire within fire, desire in deity.
>
>   (4/6, ll. 9–14)

---

[18] Joan Rees has an excellent general comment on Rossetti's significance as a poet: A slight shift of position, and what has been taken as an emblem of salvation becomes a mark of damnation. This is the central moral insight of Rossetti's work' (*Poetry of Rossetti*, 101).

[19] In identifying the sonnets I always give two numbers: the first being the number in the 1870 volume, the second the number in 1881. The one exception is for this sonnet, the so-called 6a (a number which indicates that Rossetti removed it from the sequence printed in 1881, though later editors, perceiving its centrality, have always restored it).

After those lines, the movement to the third person in 'Nuptial Sleep', a modulation from major to minor, comes as a shock, since it conveys the impression of incredible detachment on the part of the speaker, whom we associate with the lover. That shock is the rhetorical equivalent of the 'wonder' recorded at the end of the sonnet. There—following an experience of ecstatic physical union—the beloved appears to the eyes of the lover as a unique identity, wholly individuated despite the previous moments of mutual absorption. The lover's (actual) 'wonder' is thus reduplicated, or realized, in the rhetoric of the speaker, who is as it were spellbound before his imagination of the separate lovers. 'Nuptial Sleep' argues, in other words, that the heart of this work's 'poignant thirst | And exquisite hunger' ('Bridal Birth', 1/2) is an ecstasy which culminates not in the extinction but in the establishment of individual identities through love. This argument is clinched by the tense-shift executed between the sonnets, which transfers to identity and self-consciousness the values associated, both traditionally and in the previous sonnet(s), with intense feeling: immediateness, and spontaneity.

But the achievement in the sonnet is tenuous and fragile, and finally self-conflicted. Lover observes beloved much as the young man in 'Jenny' observes, lovingly, the sleeping prostitute; and the perspective is here explicitly revealed as the perspective of art and poetry. This 'wonder' matches passivities to passivities, and thus contradicts the poem's own developing energetic impulses. Furthermore, although the watery medium of sleep and dreams does not here directly threaten the sonnet's ideal of self-identity, those forms prefigure the conditions of loss later realized in 'Willowwood'.

As in 'Hand and Soul', then, the apparitions here are images of the artist's 'soul', or that to which he is ultimately committed. That is to say, the sonnet raises up an imagining of self-identity achieved through artistic practice. As *The House of Life* gradually delineates the features of that soul, however, a hollowed-out figure emerges from the expectant shadows of Beauty. For the story told by the sequence is that the images are insubstantial: literally, that the supreme moment of 'Nuptial Sleep' was a supreme fiction only. In this respect *The House of Life* is the story of betrayed hopes; and if that were all it had to tell us, it would scarcely deserve to hold more than our minimal interest. As we shall see, however, what Rossetti's work ultimately reveals are not its betrayals but its self-betrayals.

The instabilities we glimpse in 'Nuptial Sleep' initiate the sequence of illusions that form the ground of the work's conclusive nightmares. These will culminate in the terror of 'He and I' (47/98), the definitive representation of identity-loss in the sequence.

> Whence came his feet into my field, and why?
>   How is it that he sees it all so drear?
>   How do I see his seeing, and how hear
> The name his bitter silence know it by?
> This was the little fold of separate sky
>   Whose pasturing clouds in the soul's atmosphere
>   Drew living light from one continual year:
> How should he find it lifeless? He, or I?
>
> Lo! this new Self now wanders round my field,
>   With plaints for every flower, and for each tree
> A moan, the sighing wind's auxiliary:
> And o'er sweet waters of my life, that yield
>   Unto his lips no draught but tears unsealed,
>   Even in my place he weeps. Even I, not he.   (47/98)

The sonnet operates through the simple contradiction of first- and third-person pronouns, both of which are 'identified with' the poet. They are the residua of the first and third person narrators whose careers in *The House of Life* we initially traced in 'The Kiss' and 'Nuptial Sleep'. Here they emerge as the obverse and reverse of a single self-conflicted figure, the schizoid form of a disintegrated identity which has lost itself in a house of mirrors.[20]

Pronouns, those ultimate shifters, figure largely in Rossetti's sonnet-sequence. The iconographical status of 'He and I', however, contrasts with the more fluid pronominal ambiguities which play themselves out in most of the earlier sonnets. This happens because Rossetti depicts first the process and then the achievement, first 'Change' and then 'Fate'. 'He and I' is the 'Fate' that awaits Rossettian 'Change', an entropic nightmare immortalized in one dead deathless sonnet.

'Life-in-Love' is very different, a not untypical instance of Rossettian deconstruction observed in a 'changing' phase.

> Not in thy body is thy life at all,
>   But in this lady's lips and hands and eyes;
>   Through these she yields thee life that vivifies
> What else were sorrow's servant and death's thrall.

[20] See Henry Treffry Dunn, *Recollections of Dante Gabriel Rossetti and His Circle, or Cheyne Walk Life*, ed. Rosalie Mander (Westerham, Kent, 1984), 14: 'Mirrors and

Look on thyself without her, and recall
   The waste remembrance and forlorn surmise
   That lived but in a dead-drawn breath of sighs
Of vanished hours and hours eventual.

Even so much life hath the poor tress of hair
   Which, stored apart, is all love hath to show
   For heart-beats and for fire-heats long ago;
Even so much life endures unknown, even where,
   'Mid change the changeless night environeth,
   Lies all that golden hair undimmed in death.   (16/36)

The second-person pronoun here slides from ambiguity to ambiguity.
Isolated thus, in solitary quotation, we register the simple alternative that it may be taken to refer either to 'the poet' (alias D. G.
Rossetti) or to the 'old love' (alias Elizabeth Siddal Rossetti), with
'this lady' standing as the 'new love' (alias Jane Morris.)[21] The
'meaning' in each case is that both 'poet' and 'old love' are resur-
rected in the experience of 'new love', which revivifies and redeems
what would otherwise be encorpsed for ever.

Were we to restore the sonnet to its larger (1881) context in the
sequence, we should observe a further fall into ambiguity; for it is
impossible to read 'Life-in-Love' after the preceding sonnet, 'The
Lamp's Shrine', and not respond to the inertia of the latter's second-
person pronouns, which all refer to the allegorical figure 'Lord
Love'. Finally, because Rossetti rhymes this sonnet with the soon to
follow 'Death-in-Love', yet another nominal presence comes to fill
the shifting pronoun, and even names itself: 'I am Death'.

In this case, the fact that 'The Lamp's Shrine' was only added to
The House of Life in 1881 reduces by one the number of substantive
options in the 1870 sequence, but its addition also calls attention to
the unstable and shifting form of the work as a whole. In Rossetti's
lifetime *The House of Life* appeared in no less than four relatively
coherent forms: as a sequence of 16 sonnets; as a sequence of 50
sonnets and 11 songs; as a sequence of 25 sonnets and 5 songs; and
as a sequence of 101 sonnets. Rossetti treated that last as the finished

looking-glasses of all shapes, sizes and design lined the walls. Whichever way I looked
I saw myself gazing at myself.'

[21] I refer here to the traditional 'biographical' level of exegesis, which plots the
poem as a story of Rossetti's relations with Elizabeth Siddal (the Old Love) and Jane
Morris (the New Love). For a critical survey of the biographical readings see William
E. Fredeman, 'Rossetti's "In Memoriam": An Elegiac Reading of *The House of Life*',
Bulletin of the John Rylands Library, 47 (Mar., 1965), 311–17.

sequence even though it lacked the crucial sonnet 'Nuptial Sleep'.[22] Today, as for many years, most readers enter the work through the 102-sonnet version, where 'Nuptial Sleep', sequenced with the appropriately unstable number 5/6a, is restored.

And indeed this ambiguous presence of 'Nuptial Sleep' in *The House of Life* is singularly appropriate, for only in that sonnet is the work's ultimate ideal of self-identity through love defined. That Rossetti repeatedly unsettled the forms of the sequence emphasizes the work's overall lack of resolution, but that he should have removed 'Nuptial Sleep' from his last imagination of the work is a truly remarkable revelation of his loss of faith in the identity he set out to fashion and represent. Needless to say, this surrender of faith, this betrayal, is the ambiguous sign under which the work will triumph.

V

Poems (1870) is the first chapter in Rossetti's history of ultimate dissolution/disillusion. But the book is more than the record of a personal and psychic catastrophe, it is the portrait of an age. We glimpse this most clearly, if also most simply, when we recall that the book is full of various social and political poems with distinct, if obliquely presented, points of contemporary reference. 'The Burden of Nineveh', an unusually direct work, involves an ironic meditation on England's imperial imagination. This fact is glossed in the multiple pun of the title. At the proof stage Rossetti set an explanatory headnote under that title to emphasize his word-play: 'BURDEN. Heavy calamity; the chorus of a song.—*Dictionary*.'[23] Rossetti directs us to read the poem as a 'burden' in the Old Testament prophetic sense, with a relevance for England emphasized by the storied names (Thebes, Rome, Babylon, Greece, Egypt) called in the poem's roll. Finally, that Nineveh is also 'a burden to' England, an example of the self-destructive imperialism under which she currently labours, is made all but explicit at the poem's conclusion. It is particularly apt, in Rossetti's book, that the poem's focus of decadence should be the British Museum, the repository of the nation's cultural treasures.

---

[22] The 25-sonnet, 5-song version is the MS Rossetti made of the poems he wrote in 1870–1. He made a gift of it to Jane Morris, the person who had inspired most of the work. The MS (Bodleian Library) was printed (most of it) in *The Kelmscott Love Sonnets of Dante Gabriel Rossetti*, ed. John Robert Wahl (Capetown, 1954).

[23] The following discussion depends heavily upon a study of the MS and proof-material in the Ashley Library (British Museum) and the Fitzwilliam Museum.

Rossetti's poem reflects the excitement of cultural imperialism with a special force because the British Museum, at that time, was relatively small, so that recent acquisitions of Near Eastern treasure were peculiarly visible and celebrated occurrences. 'The Burden of Nineveh' draws out the implications of what Byron, sixty years earlier, had already sketched in *The Curse of Minerva*.

But this is a unique poem in a book which generally proceeds by careful, not to stay stealthy, indirection. 'Troy Town' generates an entire network of references to that fabled history of a civilization which, according to the myth, found destruction through indulgence and illicit love. This Troy theme plays a key role in linking *The House of Life* poems to the less personal material, as Rossetti must have realized: through all the proof-stages 'Troy Town' was the opening poem. In that position it would have emphasized more strongly the book's social dimensions. But at the last minute Rossetti replaced it with 'The Blessed Damozel'.

Changes of that and other kinds are the hallmark of Rossetti's discontented book. This is why, from a social point of view, the steps that Rossetti takes to marginalize his 'social themes' are in the end more important, more significant, than the themes themselves. They remind us that works like 'Troy Town' are in themselves even more obliquely mediated, as pieces of social commentary, than *The Idylls of the King*. What should be attended to, here and throughout *Poems* (1870), is not any of the book's 'ideas' but what the book is *doing* and being made to do, how carefully its materials are managed, packaged, and polished. Unlike Swinburne's deliberately outrageous *Poems and Ballads*, Rossetti does everything in his power to make sure his book will *behave*.

This manic sense of decorum makes the book not more 'crafted' but more 'crafty'. It is a monument to its own shame, a kind of whited sepulchre. We can see how this comes about if we trace the structure of change in Rossetti's book. We begin by reflecting once again on those distintegrative mechanisms observed earlier. One notes for instance that they are heavily 'languaged', so to speak, and that the extreme level of the verbal artifice is a mode that holds off, brackets out, 'reality'. All is arranged so that what occurs seems to occur at the level of the signs alone, as a play of signifiers and signifieds. No names are given, no definite events are alluded to, no places, no times, no 'referential' concretions of any kind—other than the (1870) book in which *The House of Life* is printed. Many of the works in that book have points of reference, as we have seen, but not *The House of Life* poems, which occupy the abstract space first clearly delineated in 'The Blessed Damozel'. Yet, paradoxically, these sonnets and songs comprise the most 'personal' work in the entire volume.

The book itself, in other words, provides the key referential point which alone really clarifies what is happening in *The House of Life*. The claustrophobia and abstraction of the sonnets have often been observed, but if we consider the sequence wholly in itself, we should have to see it simply as an event in language. By printing and publishing the work when and how he did, Rossetti provided the local habitation which could give social and ethical names—rather than merely technical ones—to the sonnets.

In simplest terms—they are critical for Rossetti—the act of printing and publishing establishes the 'trade associations' of his work. These associations are, however, what he wants to avoid or cancel out, in order to 'prove' that art occupies a transcendental order. Rossetti wants to establish what the Romantics called 'the truth of imagination', but *Poems* (1870) ends by showing instead how that 'truth' is rather 'an imagination' of imagination—and an imagining which, when carried out in the world, can have disastrous consequences. The book's most prominent sign of disaster is psychic disintegration, but the social significances of that sign are never far to seek. Perhaps the greatest 'moral' of Rossetti's book, for instance, could be expressed as follows: that active moves to escape 'trade associations'—to evade or avoid them rather than to oppose, in concrete and positive ways, the compromised 'world' they represent—inevitably involve a complicity with that world. It was a truth Rossetti glimpsed early in 'St. Agnes of Intercession', but in *Poems* (1870) it is fully exposed. Indeed, it is executed. In the horrors of his book Rossetti carried out the (concealed) truth of imagination for his age: that it has a truth, that it serves the world even in fleeing the world, that the truth is both a dream and a nightmare, and that it destroys the individual.

The marvel of Rossetti's work is that he chose to follow his own '*inner* standing-point' in declaring those contradictory truths, that he submitted to their 'execution'. We therefore trace the choices made by his work even in what must seem (for Rossetti) the least likely of places, the early reviews. One observes initially that they mirror the contradictions exposed in Rossetti's book. Whether written by friends or enemies, accomplices or neutral observers, two lines of understanding are repeated. *Poems* (1870) is a celebration of art, on one hand, or of love on the other; and to the degree that a mediation of the two is carried out, the book is said to be devoted to Beauty. But the mediating concept of Beauty merely resituates the contradictory registrations elsewhere. Thus, the book can be alternately seen as a manifesto of 'fleshliness' and eroticism, or of 'mysticism' and spirituality. The contradictions are multiplied: what many find laboured and obscure others see as crafted and sharply defined; and so the descriptive terms proliferate: abstract, ornate, pictorial, self-conscious, impersonal, and so forth.

These varied responses are the integrals of Rossetti's differential achievements. So much finish at the surface, so much apparent control—in a work that is also, plainly, nervous and highly unstable. Rossetti's perpetual acts of revision at every level, in the months immediately preceding publication, are but a dramatic instance of the book's consummate lack of resolution. The book shifts and changes as it seeks its ideal of articulation, that monochord of which audience approval is the tonic, reciprocity the dominant. It is a mad, an inhuman ideal—what Marx ironically called 'the soul of the commodity': a form crafted so as to be universally irresistible. It is the nineteenth-century revenant of Dante's *summum bonum*, an encorpsed form of what was once alive.

Rossetti was more deeply complicit with his immediate institutions of reception than appears even from his attempt to manage the reviews. This became most obvious when the voices of negation began to be heard, the critical notices which culminate in Buchanan's famous review. Its date of publication—well over a year after the initial appearance of *Poems* (1870)—is quite important, because it tells us how far Rossetti identified himself with Buchanan. 'The Stealthy School of Criticism' shouts back at the champion of late Victorian moral and poetic order, but it does not challenge that order, or argue that Rossetti's book challenged it. Furthermore, the poem particularly singled out by Buchanan for denunciation, 'Nuptial Sleep', which was also the key sonnet of *The House of Life*, was removed from the sequence by Rossetti when he published his new (and otherwise augmented) version of the work in 1881. Like the young painter in 'St. Agnes of Intercession', Rossetti despised and sneered at the 'poet-critic' who attacked his work, but Rossetti too, in the end, deferred.

It is an illuminating act of bad faith and betrayal, reminding us of the fear and trembling in which Rossetti worked out his damnation. We might wish that he had done otherwise, that he had braved it and defied his critics. But in fact he took the better part, for the shame of that betrayal is an eloquent sign of the ambiguous situation Rossetti's book has exposed. Buchanan is what Shelley would have called 'The Phantasm of Rossetti' in a play where Prometheus does not appear as a character. What is Promethean in *Poems* (1870) is not 'Rossetti' but what Rossetti has done. Assuming the inner standing-point throughout, the book dramatizes Rossetti's enslavement to the commercial culture he despises. That culture thereby grows again in Rossetti's book, like some terrible virus in a laboratory dish. *Poems* (1870) is a coin 'whose face reveals | The soul,—its converse, to what Power 'tis due'.

Rossetti's work set out to prove the Victorian theory of cultural touchstones which Arnold was developing elsewhere in his ideological prose: to prove that Ideal Beauty was transcendent. His achievement was to have shown that the theory was a confidence-trick which Victorian society played on itself. Thus, the clear path to fulfilment sketched in 'Hand and Soul' becomes, in the empirical testing of that prediction which Rossetti's work carried out, a field of endless wandering—in Rossetti's recurrent figuration, a maze.[24] Similarly, the Beatricean vision which was to mediate the quest for perfection continually shifted out of focus, or turned into nightmare forms.

The characteristic experience here is to be found in various pictures which Rossetti, obsessively overpainting, turned into palimpsests and cryptic surfaces. Somewhere beneath the face of Alexa Wilding hovered the unseen head of Fanny Cornforth, or Elizabeth Siddal would float about the canvas occupied by the face of Jane Morris. Rossetti fled his haunted and haunting canvases and sought relief in poetry, which for a brief time seemed open to pure forms, transparent expressions. But the hope turned to illusion as his poetry delivered up its secret and invisible texts to the fire of his art. In the 1870s, as he plunged deeper into that abyss of Beauty, neither poetry nor painting offered any sustaining fantasies of escape.

'Untruth was never yet the husk of . . . truth', Rossetti argues at the conclusion to 'The Stealthy School of Criticism' (i. 488) as he makes a final dismissal of the various deceits of Robert Buchanan.

---

[24] The central 'maze' poem by Rossetti is 'Troy Town', whose title means (at one level) a labyrinth (see *OED*).

Perhaps that relation of truth to untruth never held before, but the observation—the metaphor—is wonderfully apt for Rossetti's work, which tells the truth of false appearances, the truth that is in the husks of beauty and truth. Rossetti's poetry crucifies itself on its own infernal machineries. These always want to appear otherwise, as benevolences, but for the sake of truth Rossetti chose an unusual and lonely path: to will a suspension of disbelief in those inherited lies of art. Thence the nightmares of paradise appear in his work in their many forms, the most critical being called, commonly, Love and Art. They are dangerous and deceitful names, like the realities they denote, and in Rossetti's work none—neither names nor realities— are ever just what they seem.

This is an art difficult to practise, the index of a world not easy to survive. Rossetti allegorized both in a dramatic figure which became familiar to us only much later. It appears in another of Rossetti's notebooks, an entry of uncertain date, though it was clearly written a few years later than the passage I quoted at the outset. This time Rossetti copies a passage from Petronius and then translates it to his own verse.

> I saw the Sibyl at Cumae
> (One said) with my own eye
> She hung in a cage to read her runes
> To all the passers-by
> Said the boys 'What wouldst thou Sibyl?'
> She answered 'I would die'![25]

That scene of cultural desperation Eliot later made famous as the epigraph to a poem about another wasted world. To find it written almost fifty years before in a Rossetti notebook will surprise us only if we read as twentieth century literary historians, that is to say, if we continue to misunderstand what Rossetti's poetry is actually about.

[25] W. M. Rossetti printed these lines in 1911; his text differs slightly from the Notebook's (II, fo. 12^v).

CHAPTER 4

The *Cantos* of Ezra Pound, the Truth in Contradiction

Repression does not . . . abolish the existence of the repressed element which continues as a contradiction, often invisible, in the social fact. As such, it continues to wage the class struggle of consciousness. The history of Anglo-American literature under capitalism is the history of this struggle.

RON SILLIMAN, 'Disappearance of the Word, Appearance of the World'

BYRON'S life became a scandal in his own age, and remained so for many people for a long time afterwards. The scandal of his *work*, on the other hand, began in earnest only towards the end of his career. Thence it flourished through the age of Victoria as well as that equally high-toned aftermath we call Modernism. That his *life* was not *truly* scandalous we know because it never ceased to fascinate— never ceased to build its huge library of biographical studies. But his poetry was generally shunned by those two fastidious cultures which succeeded the Regency. Pious imaginations, whether moral or poetic, prefer to read what they think is good for them.

The case of Blake is somewhat different, for his work is a scandal in his own time. Though we call it the Romantic period, 1789–1824 was a worldly age. Indeed, Romanticism fed upon and grew fat in that worldliness. Yet Blake was its most scandalous figure, for not even the saints of the time, Southey and Coleridge for example, could take seriously the imaginations of a man who saw angels, and who claimed that to be inspired, to write from the dictation of beings who lived in eternity, was a 'litteral' truth, and not metaphor or poetic convention.

As for Rossetti, his work is still a scandal. The Fleshly School controversy which erupted around him was never in itself very serious. Rossetti went mad, but Buchanan did not drive him to it. He went mad from having looked too long into the heart of vacancy—

his own and that of his age. He put down what he saw in *The House of Life*, a vision of hell which English and American readers have learnt to avoid. Hell is more easily observed across a channel, in any other country where, perhaps, flowers of evil may be taken for things of beauty.

But the scandals surrounding the work of these men are as nothing compared to the scandal of Ezra Pound's *Cantos*. We are amused to think that anyone ever felt Byron might have been mad, bad, and dangerous to know. We are not amused by the *Cantos*. Like Pound's letters and so much of his prose, the *Cantos* is difficult to like or enjoy. It is a paradigm of poetic obscurity because its often cryptic style is married to materials which are abstruse, learned, even pedantic. The poem also makes a mockery of poetic form; and then there are those vulgar and bathetic sinkings which it repeatedly indulges through its macaronic turns of voice.

All that is scandalous, but the worst has not been said. For the *Cantos* is a fascist epic in a precise historical sense.[1] Its racism and anti-Semitism are conceived and pursued in social and political terms at a particular point in time and with reference to certain state policies. Those policies led to a holocaust for which the murder of six million Jews would be the ultimate exponent. That is truly scandalous.

For anyone convinced that works of imagination are important to human life, however, the scandal takes a last, cruel twist. Pound's *magnum opus* is one of the greatest achievements of Modern poetry in any language. That is more a shocking than a controversial idea. It shocks because it is outrageous to think so; but it is in fact a commonplace judgement passed on the poem by nearly every major writer and poet of this century. The greatness of the *Cantos* was as apparent to Pound's contemporaries as it has been to his inheritors, to his enemies as to his friends, to those who have sympathized with Pound's ideas and to those who have fought against them.

The problem of the *Cantos* locates a more general problem about works of imagination which clerical minds do not like to face. It was exposed for our modern world most trenchantly by Hazlitt in 1816 when he was lecturing on *Coriolanus*.

---

[1] See John Lauber, 'Pound's *Cantos*: A Fascist Epic', *The Journal of American Studies*, 12 (1978), 3–21; Victor C. Ferkiss, 'Ezra Pound and American Fascism', *The Journal of Politics*, 17 (1955), 173–97. The most comprehensive exploration of this subject appeared too late for me to profit from it in this writing; I mean Robert Casillo, *The Genealogy of Demons: Anti-Semitism, Fascism, and the Myths of Ezra Pound* (Evanston, 1988).

The language of poetry naturally falls in with the language of power. The imagination is an exaggerating and exclusive faculty: it takes from one thing to add to another: it accumulates circumstances to give the greatest possible effect . . . The understanding is a dividing and measuring faculty: it judges of things not according to their immediate impression on the mind, but according to their relations to one another. The one is a monopolising faculty . . . the other is a distributive faculty. . . . The one is an aristocratical and the other a republican faculty. The principle of poetry is a very anti-levelling principle. It aims at effect. . . . It has its altars and its victims, sacrifices, human sacrifices. . . . 'Carnage is its daughter'.[2]

This statement is an implicit plea for a literature of knowledge rather than a literature of power—or rather, a plea that the literature of power, poetry, find a way of accommodating itself to the demands of justice and consciousness. Hazlitt here is subjecting the entire ground of his work—specifically, his judgement that Wordsworth is the most important poet of the age—to a critical revolution. The inquiry will not lead him to an apostasy from Wordsworth. It *will* lead him to develop critical ideas which we now usually associate with Keats and the concept of 'negative capability'.

Some of the best work on Pound has been done in recent years by readers who do not shrink from the carnage which his work embodies.[3] The concept of negative capability has been specifically invoked as a vehicle for exposing the structures of contradiction which abound in the *Cantos*.[4] But this Keatsian principle, even in its Hazlittian (that is to say, in its socially conscious) salient, will finally prove too fragile for a work like Pound's. For at the back of Wordsworth's idea that the carnage of war is the daughter of a just God are those struggles of France, ultimately Napoleonic France, with England and her monarchical allies. Those circumstances encouraged a negative capability toward the parties involved. The equivocal contests in Europe between 1789 and 1815 discovered

[2] *Complete Works of William Hazlitt*, ed. P. P. Howe (London, 1930–4) iv. 214–15.

[3] See Michael A. Bernstein, *The Tale of the Tribe: Ezra Pound and the Modern Verse Epic* (Princeton, 1980); Ian F. A. Bell (ed.), *Ezra Pound: Tactics for Reading* (London, 1982), especially the essays by Peter Brooker, David Murray, and H. N. Schneidau; Martin Kayman, *The Modernism of Ezra Pound* (London, 1986); Jean Michel Rabate, *Language, Sexuality, and Ideology in Ezra Pound's Cantos* (Albany, NY, 1986); Andrew Parker, 'Ezra Pound and the Economy of Anti-Semitism', in Jonathan Arac (ed.), *Postmodernism and Politics* (Minneapolis, 1986), 70–90; Richard Sieburth, 'In Pound We Trust: The Economy of Poetry/The Poetry of Economics', *Critical Inquiry*, 14 (Autumn 1987), 142–72.

[4] Alan Durant, *Ezra Pound: Identity in Crisis* (Brighton, 1981).

those equivocal responses which have been preserved in the living memory of Romantic art.

The same is not the case with Pound's *Cantos*. Sympathizing, as I think one can and should, with so much in the poem's indictment of the Europe (and America) of 1914–38, ultimately one's powers of sympathy—one's negative capabilities—come to a halt. The poem has entered, we soon discover, a world of evil that is too terrible for a Romantic sympathy or imagination. Yeats's father, that exemplary aesthete and Romantic, glimpsed this truth about the *Cantos* very early and tried to warn his son away from becoming too deeply involved with the demonic Pound:

The poets loved of Ezra Pound are tired of Beauty, since they have met it so often. . . . I am tired of Beauty my wife, says the poet, but here is that enchanting mistress Ugliness. With her I will live, and what a riot we shall have. Not a day shall pass without a fresh horror. Prometheus leaves his rock to cohabit with the Furies.[5]

This is extraordinarily prescient, and wonderfully expressed. But what Yeats's father saw in 1918 as Ugliness would eventually reveal itself in more frightful—in unspeakable—guises. Having, against his father's judgement, put himself to school to Pound, Yeats began to cultivate poetical relations with that mistress whom Jack Butler Yeats saw as the young American's wicked new beloved. 'A terrible beauty is born', Yeats declared as he began to explore his own visions of Prometheus cohabiting with the Furies. But his words— his experience—fall far short of the realities which Pound was bent upon pursuing. That elegant oxymoron of 'A terrible beauty' is a Romantic phrase embodying a Romantic judgment; as such, it is wholly inadequate to the contradictions which are brought forth through Pound's *Cantos*.

II

Let us approach those contradictions cautiously. We begin by re-calling Pound's famous (1927) letter to *his* father in which he gave Homer Pound the 'outline of main scheme—or whatever it is' which would structure the long poem he had embarked upon:

[5] Letter from J. B. Yeats to his son, 12 Mar. 1918, cited in Richard Ellman, 'Ez and Old Billyum', in Eva Hesse (ed.), *New Approaches to Ezra Pound* (London, 1969), 60.

1. Rather like, or unlike subject and response and counter subject in fugue.

A. A. Live man goes down into world of Dead

C. B. The 'repeat in history'

B. C. The 'magic moment' or moment of metamorphosis, bust thru from quotidien into 'divine or permanent world.' Gods, etc.[6]

This is essentially the same 'scheme' which he outlined about two years later at Rapallo for Yeats, who reported as follows:

it will, when the hundredth Canto is finished, display a structure like that of a Bach Fugue. There will be no plot, no chronicle of events, no logic of discourse, but two themes, the descent into Hades from Homer, a metamorphosis from Ovid, and mixed with these mediaeval or modern historical characters.[7]

Yeats was interested in this 'scheme' because in his reading of the first twenty-seven cantos he had been troubled and confused. 'I have often found there some scene of distinguished beauty but have never discovered why all the suits could not be dealt out in some quite different order' (*Packet*, 2). Yeats was never entirely persuaded by Pound's schema, and he even confessed that he agreed 'philosophic- ally' (*L* 739) with Wyndham Lewis's critique of the new art of Joyce and Pound, that 'If we reject . . . the forms and categories of intellect there is nothing left but sensation, "eternal flux" ' (*Packet*, 2 n.). But his 'philosophical' sense was not able to resist entirely what Joyce and Pound were doing in their work and he determined to try to sympathize with the *Cantos*:

It is almost impossible to understand the art of a generation younger than one's own. I was wrong about 'Ulysses' when I had read but some first few fragments, and I do not want to be wrong again—above all in judging verse. Perhaps when the sudden Italian spring has come I may have discovered what will seem all the more [in the *Cantos*], because the opposite of all that I have attempted, unique and unforgetable. (*Packet*, 4.)

Yeats's uncertainty about the *Cantos* was, as we know, matched by Pound's. 'The whole damn poem is rather obscure, especially in fragments' was how he opened the 'fugue' letter to his father, and his descriptive 'scheme' likewise begins on a hesitant note: the poem is

[6] *The Letters of Ezra Pound 1907–1941*, ed. D. D. Paige (London, 1951), 285 (hereafter cited in the text as *L*).

[7] *A Packet for Ezra Pound* (Cuala Press, 1929), 2 (hereafter cited in text as *Packet*).

'Rather like, or unlike' the form of a fugue. As the years passed
and the work accumulated, Pound swung back and forth in his
confidence about its ultimate form. In the end he decided it was a
failure, and he lapsed into the stony silence of the final years. The
Poem finished as it had begun in 1915–27, before Pound had formulated the first of his 'grand schemes' of the work, in a nervous
swirl of fragmentary pieces.[8]

But Pound was as deceived about the *Cantos* at the end as much as
he was at the beginning. The poem had not failed, though it *was* a
record of failure and self-deception. The fugal scheme is not strictly
applicable, as Pound's vacillation in his use of it suggests; and all
those other schemes he formulated were at worst mere blustering, at
best shots in the dark.

Take those 'two themes' which he singled out, the descent into
hell and the Ovidian metamorphosis. These do in fact appear, not
merely at the outset as Cantos I and II respectively, but recurrently
through the poem as Pound's 'repeat in history'. The poem plunges
into Hades with Odysseus in Canto I, and the descent is explicitly a
figure of a quest for knowledge, a mission to consult with Tiresias,
the man 'Who even dead, yet hath his mind entire' (XLVII. 236).[9] His
message is: 'Odysseus | Shalt return through spiteful Neptune, over
dark seas, | Lose all companions' (I. 4–5)

The words are well known, a supreme text in western culture; but
what do they actually mean here in Pound's poem, what do they
signify in this latest 'Repeat in history'? Pound was, like his friend
Yeats, uncertain. The words themselves, if we consider them merely
as a linguistic event, and set aside their historical relevance, send out
a cryptic and equivocal message, for they seem to promise both
comfort (the 'return' home) and loneliness ('Lose all companions').
Even that reading hangs fire, however, especially when we remember
the deceptiveness of the source: an uncertain oracle (is it Tiresias,
Homer's *Odyssey*, or Pound's Canto I?) whose pronouncements are
subject to many constructions, including misconstructions. Beginning
from an oracle is not propitious.

While such an ominous note is not clearly struck in Canto I, it is

[8] See R. Peter Stoicheff, 'The Composition and Publication History of Ezra
Pound's *Drafts and Fragments*', *Twentieth Century Literature*, 32 (1986), 78–94.

[9] The text of the *Cantos* used throughout is the latest reprinting from Faber/New
Directions (the 10th, 1986), which contains some new material, and especially texts of
the 'forbidden cantos', LXXII and LXXIII.

difficult to miss, if it is still only half sounded, in Canto XLVII when the same Homeric text is recalled, this time through the figure of Circe:

> This sound came in the dark
> First must thou go the road
> > to hell
> And to the bower of Ceres' daughter Proserpine,
> Through overhanging dark, to see Tiresias,
> Eyeless that was, a shade, that is in hell
> So full of knowing that the beefy men know less than he,
> Ere thou come to thy road's end.
> > Knowledge the shade of a shade
> Yet must thou sail after knowledge
> Knowing less than drugged beasts. (XLVII. 236)

Circe's message is even more ominous than Tiresias'; and when we recall the hell into which the *Cantos* make their descent, the contradictoriness of the work becomes especially clear.

Cantos XIV–XVI were to represent the rottenness of the British Empire, 'the foetor of England' where 'evil [is] without dignity and without tragedy' (*L* 247–8). The cantos move via Dante into a place where all light is muted, and where a series of obscene and fragmented images stagger along. Pound's narrative in these 'Hell Cantos' recall plates 17–20 of *The Marriage of Heaven and Hell* and various parts of *The [First] Book of Urizen*, and they were to have a powerful influence on such later works as Ginsberg's *Howl*.[10]

But Eliot's critical comments on these visions, which he published in *After Strange Gods* (1934), point toward something important and even more troubling in this poetry: 'Mr. Pound's Hell . . . is a perfectly comfortable one for the modern mind to contemplate, and disturbing to no one's complacency: it is a Hell for the *other* people, the people we read about in the newspapers, not for oneself and one's friends'.[11] The descent into hell is associated in Pound's work with knowledge, and he certainly thought these cantos contained a

---

[10] Pound specifically alludes to Blake at the outset of Canto XVI; Carroll F. Terrell in his indispensable *Companion to the Cantos of Ezra Pound* (Berkeley, 1980, 1984), i. 69, gives only a vague general citation here. Pound's text shows that he is thinking specifically about certain plates in *The [First] Book of Urizen* and *The Marriage of Heaven and Hell*. For Pound's later influence see the work of Marjorie Perloff, especially *The Poetics of Indeterminacy: Rimbaud to Cage* (Princeton, 1981) and *The Dance of Intellect: Studies in the Poetry of the Pound Tradition* (Cambridge, 1985).

[11] *After Strange Gods* (London, 1934), 43.

revelation of truths which most people would not face or did not know. But so far as Pound's project is concerned, Eliot touched a crucial problem: the hell of the *Cantos* does not appear to yield up an unknown world, and the poem does not go there to acquire knowledge. It goes there to preach. 'I am perhaps didactic,' Pound said of these cantos, but he brushed the criticism aside:

It is all rubbish to pretend that art isn't didactic. A revelation is always didactic. Only the aesthetes since 1880 have pretended the contrary. (*L* 248.)

Pound is correct—in principle. Unfortunately, his remarks call attention to the contradictions in his understanding of what a descent into hell means for a poem which is itself questing after knowledge. Perhaps, as we shall see, there is a revelation in the 'Hell Cantos' which Pound and his poem were unable to realize in 1922.

If we consider Pound's use of Ovidian metamorphosis—the second of his work's two major 'themes'—a similar set of problems arises. According to Pound, metamorphosis was to come as a magical moment of transition 'from quotidien into "divine or permanent world"'. Metamorphosis was his poem's explicit paradisal figure, brilliantly and perhaps most famously exemplified at the opening of Canto III, where the text recalls Pound in a quotidian Venice of 1907:

> For the gondolas cost too much, that year,
> And there were not 'those girls', there was one face,
> And the Buccentoro twenty yards off, howling 'Stretti'
>
> (III. 11)

But gradually this scene changes, and a set of romantic images rises up:

> Gods float in the azure air,
> Bright gods and Tuscan, back before dew was shed.

The passage unfolds to one of those 'scenes of distinguished beauty' which so struck Yeats, and which have been the focus of interest for many readers of the *Cantos*. Here, however, it itself undergoes a metamophosis when the text abruptly shifts to the vicious world of medieval Spain via the *Cantar de myo cid*, a world of 'drear waste', 'silk tatters', and 'Ignez da Castro murdered'.

Metamorphosis in the *Cantos* appears indeed, like the descent into hell, as a 'repeat in history', but in all cases the experience of metamorphosis carries with it images of threat and destruction. In Canto II, where the theme of metamorphosis is first explicitly announced, the figure of ultimate beauty appears in a dissolving series of fearful and inspiring faces:

> Sleek head, daughter of Lir,
>   eyes of Picasso
> Under black fur-hood, lithe daughter of Ocean;
> And the wave runs in the beach-groove:
> Eleanor, ἐλέναυς and ἐλέπτολις!'
>   And poor old Homer blind, blind, as a bat,
> Ear, ear for the sea-surge, murmur of old men's voices:
> Let her go back to the ships,
> Back among Grecian faces, lest evil come on our own,
> Evil and further evil, and a curse cursed on our children,
> Moves, yes she moves like a goddess
> And has the face of a god
>   and the voice of Schoeney's daughters,
> And doom goes with her in walking.   (II. 6)

We do not have to translate or register all the allusions and word-plays in this dense passage to recognize its antithetical structure. Here is metamorphosis with, quite literally, a vengeance—a structure of metamorphosis like nothing so much as the cruel story of Actaeon, which Pound recurs to throughout the *Cantos*.

To the degree that Pound's work sets out to redefine, for the twentieth century, an order of permanent or foundational civilization, it does not merely fail, it engenders the plot of its own failure. Pound began and ended with the intention of writing such an earthly paradise. But he found his intentions constantly frustrated. 'It is difficult to write a paradiso', he told Donald Hall in 1960, 'when all the superficial indications are that you ought to write an apocalypse'.[12] But even in 1960 he wanted to call the adversative elements 'superficial', for he still had in view that 'order of ascension' in his poem which would conclude in a Paradiso.

The order of ascension was the act of writing to date (and as it turned out the date did not matter since it was endlessly repeated) in which he was 'writing to resist the view that Europe and civilisation are going to Hell' (DH 48). That formulation of the project is extremely interesting since Pound saw the passage to hell as an

---

[12] See Donald Hall, 'Ezra Pound: An Interview', *Paris Review*, 28 (1962), 47 (hereafter cited in the text as DH).

essential experience, and hardly one to be resisted. Thus we see how ambivalent the image of hell is for Pound, torn as his work was between the demands of Homer on one hand and Dante on the other. Indeed, hell in the *Cantos* is itself a metamorphic figure.

Pound's (poetic) quest for Total Form, like his (cultural) quest for the earthly paradise, survives only in its own contradictions. These are not simply metaphors, however, like Yeats's 'terrible beauty', they are ugly and furious, as Yeats's father knew. In what Pound named 'the fight for light versus sub-consciousness', he saw that the struggle 'demands obscurities and penumbras', or what he sometimes called 'my muddles' (DH 48). These sentimental formulations scarcely touch the edge of the whole truth, however. 'A lot of contemporary writing avoids inconvenient areas of the subject', Pound said, and he determined to try not to avoid those inconveniences in the *Cantos* (DH 48). That determination made him seek for a form 'elastic enough to take the necessary material. It had to be a form *that wouldn't exclude something merely because it didn't fit*' (DH 23, my italics).

That is a startling, a paradoxical idea, yet it only repeats, in a more direct way, what he had said of the *Cantos* around 1915, in one of his earliest drafts for the work: 'Let in your quirks and tweeks, and say the thing's an artform, | . . . the modern world | Needs such a rag-bag to stuff all its thoughts in'.[13] At that point Pound thought *Sordello* would be his model, but had he listened to the *tone* of his early efforts he might have realized that Byron and *Don Juan* would be even more powerful presences in his work.

III

The contradictions in the *Cantos* were finally (1936) judged by Yeats, who tried to sympathize with them, to have been 'carried beyond reason', a work of 'more deliberate nobility and the means to convey it' than any other contemporary poem, but one which is 'constantly interrupted, broken, twisted into nothing by its direct opposite, nervous obsession, nightmare, stammering confusion'. Working in this way Pound has not 'got all the wine into the bowl', for to Yeats poetic 'form must be full, sphere-like, single'.[14] The charge would

[13] The text is reproduced in Ronald Bush, *The Genesis of Ezra Pound's Cantos* (Princeton, 1976); see p. 53.

[14] 'Introduction', *The Oxford Book of Modern Verse 1892–1935* (Oxford, 1936), pp. xxiv–xxvi (hereafter cited in the text as Y*O*).

have struck home because Pound had always embraced the idea that
' "Good Writing" is perfect control'.[15]

And yet how odd does Yeats's critique now seem coming from
that great inheritor of Blake! Had the antinomian Romantic annotated the passage, he would have subjected it to the same abuse he
heaped upon Bishop Watson's 'Apology for the Bible' and Wordsworth's *Excursion*. If Pound in the *Cantos* had been 'carried beyond
reason', Blake would have applauded his condition, and if his wine
spilt from or overflowed his chalice, that too would have received
Blake's applause. Only men like Sir Joshua Reynolds, men who
knew nothing of inspiration, imagined that the soul of art was an
orderly one. 'Bring out number weight & measure in a year of
dearth'; 'The cistern contains, the fountain overflows'.[16] Blake's
work, as we have seen, is itself notably fractured and unstable—
'You shall not bring me down to believe such fitting & fitted'—and
he would have sympathized with Pound's desire to put into the
Cantos whatever could not be made to fit.

Whether he would have also recognized the sheer physical similarities between his 'composite art' and Pound's ideogrammatical
texts is not so clear. None the less, the congruities are quite plain.
Any page of the *Cantos* immediately strikes one with its material
weight and physique. This quality is most pronounced in the later
cantos (from LII to the end), at least in the texts that most readers
know. But even on pages that have no ideograms the effect is
unmistakable. Letters, words, and phrasal units are treated as
material things, so that we encounter the page both as configuration
and as discourse. The effect is produced partly by the optical appearance of a free verse form, partly by the different type-founts
required when so many languages are being used, and partly by the
recovery of various kinds of 'found' materials. None of these pages
deploy Chinese ideograms; nevertheless, they are all 'ideogrammatical'
texts.

The page itself in Pound thus becomes one of his most prominent
figures of permanence. Nothing illustrates this so well as the first
editions of the first two instalments of the *Cantos*, those two badly
neglected books privately printed as *A Draft of XVI. Cantos* (1925)
and *A Draft of the Cantos XVII–XXVII (1928)*. These texts, oversize

[15] 'The Serious Artist', in *Literary Essays of Ezra Pound*, ed. T. S. Eliot (London,
1954), 49.
[16] William Blake, *The Marriage of Heaven and Hell*, plate 7.

quartos printed on laid paper, distinctly recall—as Pound well knew[17]—the work of William Morris and the whole tradition of decorated book production which was revived in the late nineteenth century. The very title of Pound's first instalment of cantos seems to be a deliberate echo of the first instalment of Dante Gabriel Rossetti's *The House of Life* sequence. The borders and decorated capitals in Pound's texts were done by Henry Strater and Gladys Hynes, but these two artists were not allowed to work on Pound's texts as free agents. We know from their correspondence that they followed Pound's specific and detailed instructions.[18]

But while the face of these texts says one thing, their converse says something very different. They offer, initially, an appearance of finishedness and monumentality, but of course their titles move in the opposite direction. In each case we are dealing with 'A Draft of' something, or sets of texts which are in process—both on their way towards some future conclusion, and (presumably) in a present condition of intrinsic tentativeness. These early editions come to the reader in figures of immensity and permanence, yet they are both among the most transient of Pound's works. Few readers have ever seen them, and in the many reprintings of the *Cantos* these initial incarnations have been completely forgotten. The third book instalment of Pound's work, *A Draft of XXX Cantos* (1930), was also privately printed, but its format is small octavo and the splendid coloured designs in the first two books are no longer present.

There will be 'a repeat in' this early history throughout the later printing career of Pound's work.[19] For example, unless you had copies of the first instalments of Pound's poem, each new part would come to you on its own, fragmented from the whole. Cantos XXXI–XLI were published in 1934, Cantos XLII–LI in 1937, Cantos LII–LXXI in 1940, and Cantos LXXIV–LXXXIV in 1948. Only at that point (1948) did a 'collected' edition of the *Cantos* appear, and when it did the contradictory impression of monumentality and instability was once again apparent. It is a massive book, of course, but censored passages appear from time to time (these kinds of publisher's interventions began in 1940), and—most startling of

---

[17] See Pound's letter of 1924 to William Bird, and particularly his comment to Wyndham Lewis in a letter of 3 Dec. 1924 (*L* 262).

[18] Lawrence Rainey demonstrates this beyond any doubt in his forthcoming essay on Pound, 'Desperate Love'.

[19] See Barbara C. Eastman, *Ezra Pound's Cantos: The Story of the Text 1948–1975* (Orono, 1975), and Peter Makin, *Pound's Cantos* (London, 1985), ch. 16.

all—the sequence is interrupted by the complete absence of Cantos LXXII–LXXIII.

When the sections *Rock Drill* and *Thrones* were added to the work in 1955 and 1959, the *Cantos* gestured toward the achievement of some massive synthesis. But once again that gesture would prove an illusion, and its illusory nature would be exposed with the appearance, in 1970, of the final book-section, *Drafts and Fragments*. In this culminant period of the work's publishing history during Pound's lifetime, to trace the development of the many reprintings of the 'collected' editions is profoundly instructive. As each new instalment appeared after 1954, both New Directions and Faber and Faber would add it to their collected editions of the *Cantos* whenever a reprinting was called for. In addition, local changes in these texts were made from time to time, but in the most random and idiosyncratic ways, and independently by each publisher. The text kept changing before one's eyes, and the process did not stop with Pound's death. New reprintings brought the addition of yet further pieces of text, which were then added at the end of the book—or in certain instances, deleted from the book, as opinion changed about the authenticity of the texts.

The poem's incompletion thus seems duplicated and reduplicated even as it also seems unable to cease its pursuit of that illusive sense of an ending. The most recent (the tenth) reprinting (1986) by New Directions represents what Pound might well have called 'an apocalypse' of his text, for it tacks on new material at the beginning and the ending alike: a title and half-title said (in a 'Publisher's Note') to have been authorized by Pound, a concluding set of gratulant verses to Olga Rudge, and—at last—the missing Cantos LXXII–LXXIII. These cantos were first printed in Italy in 1944–5 in ephemeral fascist periodicals—they are written in Italian—and they were later reprinted in a private edition in 1983, also in Italy.[20] The text in the New Directions collected *Cantos* follows the text of 1983, but that is very different indeed from the texts of 1944–5. Furthermore, there are other texts of these cantos—typescripts—which have never been published.

The text of the *Cantos* thus turns out to be as nervous and unbalanced in its posthumous existence as it ever was during Pound's lifetime of working at it. He didn't want to 'exclude something [from

[20] See Massimo Bacigalupo, 'The Poet at War: Ezra Pound's Suppressed Italian Cantos', *The South Atlantic Quarterly*, 83 (1984), 69–79.

it] merely because it didn't fit', and as he kept avoiding such ex-
clusions himself, so his inheritors have followed after him. It is a
poem, as Yeats saw, in which there must be 'nothing to check the
flow' (YO, p. xxiv), a poem directed toward a form and order which
will only be possible through what Yeats was dismayed to call
Pound's 'loss of self-control' (YO, p. xxv).

The Cantos thereby moves into its forbidden and forbidding territ-
ories, seeks its 'sympathy for the devil'. This is no play of mask and
anti-mask, however, no marriage of heaven and hell. The Cantos is so
resolute in its will to include everything that it goes to the limit of the
known—which is to say our idea of the civilized or moral—world.
Fascism is our word for that limit, but it is only a word, a critical
abstraction. Not everything in the Cantos is fascist, of course, any
more than every part of Eichmann's life was absorbed in his activities
for the Third Reich. But when the work *is* fascist there is no mistaking the fact: for example in Canto CIV, when he presents Hitler
as a Blakean figure, 'furious from perception' (CIV 741) because he
has grasped the international Jewish conspiracy of bankers and
usurocrats; or at the opening of the first of the Pisan Cantos, in
Pound's elegiac lines for the dead Mussolini; or throughout Canto
XLI's presentation of Mussolini's economic programmes; or, perhaps
most dramatically, in the suppressed Italian Cantos, which are an
extended poetic tribute to the tradition of Italian fascist ideology
and personal character.

The poem finds the local habitations and the names for what it
signifies to be fascist. It is particular on these matters, as it should
be; for being particular is what poetry does, is what poetry is
supposed to do. Thus the particularity of Pound's fascism is matched
by the particularities of his anti-Semitism throughout the Cantos, as
numerous passages could be adduced to show. Whether the poem
should have dared these particularities, whether it should have
entered such worlds in the first place, are other questions, questions
which Yeats, for example—who more than sympathized with Pound's
actual views—decided in the negative. But to Pound, Yeats's decision
could only be one which avoided what Yeats' found to be 'inconvenient areas of the subject'.

Pound did not think that fascism was an inconvenient area of his
subject. On the contrary, Mussolini was central. But as the 'poem
including history' went on, it accumulated an array of 'heteroclite
elements' (DH 48), and if they did not easily fit together, they were

none the less, for Pound, indispensable—Homer, Frobenius, Coke and the *Institutes*, Sigismundo Malatesta, Confucius, Jefferson and Adams, the Sienese bank Monte dei Paschi, and so forth. The pursuit of paradisal knowledge became in the *Cantos* a mutant—an empiricist—reconstruction of the myth of Faust. The poem is itself a continuous descent into hell, an unending consultation with sources of truth. In the event, a metamorphosis of the entire poem also takes place. The *Cantos* turns on Pound, like Actaeon's dogs; the poem unfolds its nightmares.[21]

This great metamorphosis affects every text in the work. The prophecy of Tiresias in Canto I appears, in the context of the entire poem, an ironic forecast indeed. The Hell Cantos, so full of hate, jar against the work's later attempts to ground the poem in an ideal of love. More than that, however, those cantos turn out not to be a vision of hell at all—as Eliot had so shrewdly discerned. Or rather, they become a vision of hell in a sense utterly transformed from what the text, and Pound, had originally intended. Pound did not imagine them as a 'repeat' of the consultation with Tiresias, though they turn out to be, in part, precisely that, only the knowledge they deliver emerges in contradiction as the text turns back on itself:

> bog of stupidities,
> malevolent stupidities, and stupidities,
> the soil living pus, full of vermin . . .
>   pandars to authority,
> pets-de-loup, sitting on piles of stone books,
> obscuring the texts with philology . . .
> the air without refuge of silence,
>   the drift of lice, teething,
> and above it the mouthing of orators,
> the arse-belching of preachers . . .   (xiv. 63)

The lines give back to us fore-echoes of his post-war commentaries, both in and out of the *Cantos*, on his own life's work. Indeed, Canto XIV preaches down 'the betrayers of language' in the language of that betrayal, and the text thereby betrays itself, as Pound himself

---

[21] Hugh Kenner has an excellent discussion of the 'arrayed' structure of the poem (*The Pound Era*, London, 1975, 360–1), which he links to Buckminster Fuller's concept of synergy, or 'the behaviour of whole systems, unpredicted by the knowledge of component parts' (360). Kenner does not use these ideas to show how the *Cantos* might be fated, as it were, to undermine itself at all points by the employment of such modes. In effect, that is what I am trying to do here. For an analogous, but wholly theoretical, discussion of Pound's self-contradictions see Andrew Parker (above, n. 3).

would later show. This is not a hell for other people, as Eliot
thought, it is a hell for anyone, and for Pound as well. No names are
assigned to the damned here, as they were in Dante, only pieces of
names—cryptic letters dangling at the end of ellipses:

> . . . . e and . . . . . n, their wrists bound to
>   their ankles . . .
> And with them . . . . r.   (XIV. 61)

Pound thought this style appropriate since the damned were both
inhuman and legion.[22] But it is an invidious style which leaves no one
safe, least of all the man whose name is informed with his own
infernal letters, *ezra pound*. The text, seemingly so confident of what
it knows and sees, stands blind and unconscious of itself. The conclusion of Canto XV is therefore particularly striking:

> 'Ηέλιον τ' 'Ηέλιον
>   blind with the sunlight,
> Swollen-eyed, rested,
>   lids sinking, darkness unconscious.   (XV. 67)

The poem emerges from its understanding of Malebolge into a
language prophetic with contradictory meanings, 'blind with the
sunlight' in an entirely ironic sense.

Pound's text is thus 'carried beyond reason', beyond his own
Modernist reason as well as the Romantic reason of his friend Yeats.
Pound wishes to exclude nothing, and the poem fulfils his wish. It
descends into hells and undergoes metamorphoses, but the experiences
are born along by shadowy counter-currents. We tend to comprehend the demonic elements under the name fascism, but that is only
a name, and to most Anglo-Americans very much a hell for other
people. If the *Cantos* could speak, however, part of what it would say
is 'I myself am hell'; and if it could be read, its readers would have to
find ways of repeating those words.

Poetry must have sympathy for the devil, nor can that demon be a
beast for other people. Poems come to show the human face of what
we would rather imagine as inhuman. The *Cantos* are not vitiated or
ruined by their fascism—that is merely a sentimental way of reading
them, a way of allowing us to preserve our own confidence in the
possession of their truth. The fascism of the poem is the work's
ultimate experience of metamorphosis—for Pound, obviously, but

[22] See *L* 293, where Pound discusses these matters in a letter to John Lackey
Brown.

for us his readers as well. The poem forces us to the brink of an ultimate spiritual catastrophe that corresponds exactly to what we associate with Pound. The experience tells us that evil is what human beings bring into the world, that evil is what we do (though it is not the only thing we do). Fascism, like Ezra Pound, occupied the human world, and occupied it in a powerful, even a dominant, way. Human beings have extraordinary capacities for evil. Fascism is one way human beings decided to be human in the twentieth century, and the *Cantos* shows us how this was, how this might have been, true. Though the name for this way has gone out of fashion, it is not a way that has yet been abandoned, or that can be forgotten. It is our touchstone for reading the *Cantos*.

IV

We should like to think, perhaps, that in its quest for knowledge the poem moved in a tragic rhythm to some final anagnorisis, a culminant revelation of the error and evil to which it had been committed. The Pisan Cantos are commonly read in this way because of their subject-matter and the circumstances of their composition. Written while he was imprisoned for treason in the Disciplinary Training Center at Pisa after the defeat of the Axis powers, these cantos ruminate the disaster which had overtaken Pound's life and his most cherished ideals. They are full of nostalgia, regret, self-recrimination. One of their most attractive qualities is their loving attention to small details— personal memories and pictures from the gone world of years before, and a kind of Thoreau-like attention to immediate particularities. He will observe with great care the way a wasp builds her nest or the behaviour of a colony of ants, and he will then cast the experiences— tiny though they be—into the most splendid, and apposite, poetic forms:

> As a lone ant from a broken ant-hill
> from the wreckage of Europe, ego scriptor.   (LXXVI. 458)

But we must not be deceived by these 'scenes of distinguished beauty'. The catastrophe of the *Cantos* remains, like the hell un-covered in Canto XIV, if not entirely without dignity, then certainly without tragedy. To imagine hell as tragic forms the structure of Romantic satire when it turns to face the hypocrisy of the middle classes. That is Byron's and Blake's way of imagining, but it is neither Rossetti's nor Pound's.

When we think to read the Pisan Cantos as Pound's tragic recognition—for that matter, when we think to read the *Drafts and Fragments* that way—we might pause to remember how much remained unrecognized, to the end, by Pound. Obviously he had met with some terrible disaster, but the event left his commitments to fascism almost completely intact. During the years at St Elizabeth's Hospital he remained in close communication with American Nazis and other fascist sympathizers, whose activities and ideas he encouraged.[23] Academics like to emphasize his contacts during that period with sympathetic figures like Charles Olson, or his later interviews with Donald Hall and Allen Ginsberg. Important as these events were, there is another, bleaker truth to the matter of Pound's post-war years. Olson finally stopped going to see Pound because he could no longer bear to listen to his anti-Semitic and racist talk.

We know that Pound ultimately repudiated his anti-Semitism, but we have not been so attentive to the way that repudiation was expressed. It came during his interview with Ginsberg in 1967, when Pound surfaced briefly from the suffocating muteness of the last ten years. As Ginsberg praised the old man's achievement in the *Cantos*, Pound flinched away, called it all 'A mess . . . My writing—stupidity and ignorance all the way through', and he went on to declare that 'The intention was bad':

That's the trouble—anything I've done has been an accident—any good has been spoiled by my intentions—the preoccupation with irrelevant and stupid things. . . . But my worst mistake was the stupid, suburban prejudice of anti-Semitism, all along, that spoiled everything.[24]

We shall return to consider the question of intentional as opposed to accidental achievements. Here one must note the appalling inadequacy of Pound's reference to his anti-Semitism as a 'stupid, suburban prejudice'. Had it been a prejudice he cultivated as a small suburban shamefulness, this formulation might have sufficed. But Pound was a public figure, and he broadcast his 'prejudice' as part of an entire vision of an ideal human culture; and he placed that

[23] See especially the powerful recent study of E. Fuller Torrey, *The Roots of Treason: Ezra Pound and the Secrets of St. Elizabeth's* (London, 1984).

[24] 'Encounters with Ezra Pound', in Allen Ginsberg, *Composed on the Tongue* (Bolinas, Calif., 1980), 7, 8. Ginsberg says that the wording attributed to Pound is 'almost exact'.

vision in practical service to fascist Italy, and linked it to fascist Germany; and he did this in the *Cantos* as well as in his unspeakable radio broadcasts. To confess all this as a 'stupid, suburban prejudice' is not merely to misuse words, it is to have mistaken the issues entirely. Pound's final bitter silence, his inarticulate sense of some kind of utter failure, is far more eloquent, far more truthful.

In such a context, one ought no longer to be mistaking the way contradiction functions in Pound's *Cantos*. Perhaps the most famous text in the Pisan section, the conclusion of Canto LXXXI, is a good case in point. The incantation against 'vanity', for example, is commonly read as Pound's charge against himself, and while this reading is not merely possible but necessary, it runs parallel (or counter) to another that may have been even more to Pound's purposes:

> The ant's a centaur in his dragon world.
> Pull down thy vanity, it is not man
> Made courage or made order or made grace . . .
>   Pull down thy vanity
> Thou art a beaten dog beneath the hail,
> A swollen magpie in a fitful sun,
> Half black half white
> Nor knowst'ou wing from tail
> Pull down thy vanity
>   How mean thy hates
> Fostered in falsity,
>   Pull down thy vanity,
> Rathe to destroy, niggard in charity,
> Pull down thy vanity,
>   I say pull down.   (LXXXI. 521)

Pound here is talking about the 'Half black half white' American army who, having won the war, parade their courage, grace, and order.[25] He is talking as well about what such an army has done to Italy ('Rathe to destroy'), but most of all he is thinking of the privations to which he has been personally subjected. Hatred has been a recurrent subject in Canto LXXXI and this passage means to oppose that meanness with a positive ideal which Pound associates with active love. The generosity of the black American soldier who made Pound a table from a packing case is a figure of such love

---

[25] See Peter D'Epiro, 'Whose Vanity Must Be Pulled Down?', *Paideuma*, 13/2 (Fall, 1984), 247–52.

presented early in the canto, but Pound delivers the *figura* so as to emphasize that the act had to be performed surreptitiously lest the soldier be reprimanded by his superiors ('doan yu tell no one I made it', 519). Unlike that single black soldier, the American army is 'niggard in charity', the text declares, thus making an aural (and, incidentally, a racist) word-play back to the charitable soldier.

The touchstone for that soldier's charity is the vision that enters Pound's tent at the end of the canto, and that introduces the 'vanity' passage. It is a vision of eyes that show no anger or hatred, 'the full Εἰδὼς' of how Pound had first and last conceived his own work:

> To have gathered from the air a live tradition
> Or from a fine old eye the unconquered flame,
> This is not vanity. (522)

The eye here is explicitly that of Wilfred Scawen Blunt, but it is figuratively Pound's as well; for it is Pound who attributed to the coarse and self-important Blunt such splendid virtues, and it is Pound who made his life's work that project of preserving cultural greatness.[26]

Here and to the end of his poem Pound would confess to the vanity of his negligence, his failures to act ('error is all in the not done'). He would never inquire into, let alone penetrate, the evil in his loves:

> What thou lovest well remains,
>   the rest is dross
> What thou lov'st well shall not be reft from thee
> What thou lov'st well is thy true heritage
> Whose world, or mine or theirs
>   or is it of none?
> First came the seen, then thus the palpable
>   Elysium, though it were in the halls of hell,
>   What thou lovest well is thy true heritage
> What thou lov'st well shall not be reft from thee (521)

There is a sentimental way of reading these great lines, a way that agrees to be moved by their devotion to some ideal of love. Nor is that way entirely wrong. But it *is* mistaken, for in truth this is a frightening passage, and it will appear as such so long as we keep our minds clear about what it is, exactly, that Pound and his poem

---

[26] Terrell in the *Companion* (ii. 454) simply accepts Pound's evaluation of the colourful Blunt.

have loved so long and well. 'The full Εἰδὼς' is an 'Elysium', but its roots strike down to 'the halls of hell', nor is that hell a mere metaphor. Is it a comfort or a catastrophe that what this poem loves, what Pound loves, shall 'not be reft' away—in a word, that its fascism will stay with it for ever, as an essential part of its 'true heritage'? Surely we must see how this is a catastrophe, and we do Pound's work a profound disservice if we do not also call it that holocaust in which, like Paolo and Francesca, his work will turn for ever. What Pound loves so well 'remains' and its 'heritage' may and should be traced in its full Εἰδὼς, to the end. The rest, the illusion that his poetry—that any poetry?—is a matter of unadulterated beauty, is mere dross. Pound's text speaks a fuller truth than his mind was able to grasp, and one may well recall, in this Poundian hymn to love, the sobering alternative truths that Swinburne had earlier put into the mouth of Althaea:

> Love is one thing, an evil thing, and turns
> Choice words and wisdom into fire and air.
> And in the end shall no joy come, but grief,
> Sharp words and soul's division and fresh tears.[27]

V

These words from Swinburne's great poem bring us back to the problem of truth in poetry and—just as important—of how the reader is to deal with it. What Althaea says here about love is, in a sense Swinburne wants to make very clear, obviously *not* true. Love in *Atalanta in Calydon* is not at all 'one thing', though it *is* 'an evil thing'—whatever else it may be besides (including a good thing). In an abstract sense, therefore, the passage seems to say something about Love which is untrue. But the lines are cunning. In emphasizing the partiality of Althaea's view, as well as its blindness, Swinburne makes her speak so that we shall sympathize with that view but, at the same time, understand its limitedness. Love is many things in *Atalanta in Calydon*, some of them are evil, some of them are not.

The poem knows more than the character in the poem, and one structure of poetic truth is founded in that distinction. But because

[27] *Atalanta in Calydon* (London, 1865), 11.

ɔoems are also agents in the field of themselves,[28] they do not
ʿepresent truth, or embody knowledge, in a formally self-completed
ʌay. That idea is what Arnold, for certain historical reasons, wanted
ʿo promote—for example in his famous sonnet to Shakespeare, who
ːs Arnold's paradigm of poetic imagination because to be 'Shakespeare'
ːs to be 'Self-school'd, self-scann'd, self-honour'd, self-secure'. Arnold's
Shakespeare is Arnold's proof that poetry has the freedom of com-
ɔlete self-integrity.

There are, however, other Shakespeares, some of whom abide our
questions, some of whom even nod from time to time. Blake began,
for the modern world, a mode of poetic investigation which moved
against that view of imagination which Arnold inherited from Kant
and Coleridge. Byron and Rossetti represent two related contestatory
lines, and the *Cantos* is yet another massive counter-argument, the
most sustained to date. But it was not an argument Pound wanted to
make. His convictions were all Arnoldian. In *Guide to Kulchur*, which
calls itself 'notes for a totalitarian treatise' on art,[29] Pound suggested
that there were two kinds of imaginative work: the one, perhaps best
exemplified by Dante, he called 'totalitarian' (95) because it appears
to make a complete synthesis of its materials; the other he calls
'modern' because it is restless and unfinished, and because it records
the struggle for synthesis, but not its achievement. Pound specifically
instances the *Cantos* as an example of the latter, a work which
exhibits 'the defects inherent in a record of struggle' (135).

The *Cantos* is therefore proof, even on Pound's own showing, that
poetry may not be 'totalitarian' even when its ideology is. But the
poem develops a more compelling 'proof' by showing in concrete
detail how it is that poetry stands beyond anyone's complete possession. Consider again, for example, those much-praised lines from
Canto LXXXI: 'Pull down thy vanity, it is not man | Made courage
or made order or made grace'. Had Blake read these lines he would
have been outraged; and were he asked who made courage and
order and grace, he would have said, precisely, 'man', who for Blake
made everything—for good and for ill alike. Had one asked Byron
who made such things, he would have equivocated: 'If God exists,
God made them; but if he doesn't exist, they are the work of

[28] The phrase is adapted from a line in John Hollander's *Reflections on Espionage*
(New York, 1976), 15, where he writes (in reference to poets figured as spies): 'Each is
an agent in the field of himself.'
[29] (New York, 1952), 27. Two further citations below are given in the text.

Chance.' Rossetti would have attributed them to 'Love' in all it
contradictory aspects. For Pound, courage and order and grace ar
the creations of Nature, or what he calls here 'the green world'.

When Pound, or the *Cantos*, delivers those lines, the form of th
discourse insists that they will be read, as it were, beyond themselves
In this case such a freedom, such an openness to questioning anc
self-questioning, is licensed in the text's shrewd enjambment, whicl
places the word 'man' in two syntaxes—as the complement of th
verb 'is', and as the subject of the verb 'made'.[30] One syntax move:
to associate, the other to dissociate, the thought of 'man' from th
idea of 'vanity', so that a small contradiction is set up. That contradiction is a summons to the reader to intervene, an opening or gap ir
the poetry which demands some kind of response (initially registerec
as a choice to be made). In this way the poem sets in motion a
dialectical structure of relations which will not be held in check by
arbitrary authorities, including the arbitrary authorities of the text
itself. Interventions will be as particular as the originary acts of
production.

In the recent past critics associated these kinds of poetic structures
with the power of metaphor to generate what was often called
'ambiguity'. But Pound, like Blake, was hostile to the metaphoric
theory of imagination. Both insisted that poetry was a discourse not
of ambiguous but of determinate meanings and forms: a discourse of
particulars, of 'bounding lines', of clear distinctions. Pound, quoting
the *Odyssey* (XII. 183), invoked a phrase used by Homer to describe
the singing of the Sirens, 'Ligur' aiode'. When Pound translated it
'keen or sharp singing . . ., song with an edge on it' (*L* 285), he called
attention to its antithetical character (a discourse that is both
beautiful and dangerous, clear and deceptive). The thought here is
to gain a rich texture or poetic surface—and hence to generate
significance—by opening the discourse not to 'levels of interpretation'
but to multiplicities of response.

Such an imagination of imagination inclines to a metonymic
rather than a metaphoric engineering. It can take many forms—
Blake's, Byron's, Rossetti's, and Pound's work are all inclined to

[30] Elizabeth Helsinger suggests to me that the passage may involve a third reading
(with the enjambment working to create the adjective 'man-made'). And Leofranc
Holford-Strevens suggests that 'one might take "made" as a passive participle
agreeing with "man" and having "courage" etc, for complement (the pattern of
"Jesus Christ was God made man")'.

metonymic forms, though in other respects these poets could scarcely be more different. Poetry in this mode—allegory and satire are its greatest genres—will always tend to the accumulative and the ornamental, just as it will always tend to clarify the distance that separates itself from it audiences. This larger rhetorical structure mirrors the events which develop in the more local ways we have observed. The *Cantos* will seek the most precise expression, or what Pound idealized as the exactitude of prose: the ideogram and the image are the exponents of what he had in mind to do.

The paradoxical result of this pursuit of precision and limitedness is what one registers in the face of a sculptured form. The form's definition opens the field of itself, or—as art commentators like to say—creates the space within which it stands or moves. Wallace Stevens's 'Anecdote of a Jar' is one of the clearest statements of this kind of beauty, which Stevens called 'the beauty of inflections' (as opposed to 'the beauty of innuendoes'). The determinateness of the image sets up a gravitational field towards which everything which is not the image inclines to move; and when those othernesses move into the field, they do not implode into the initial image, but preserve their distinctness.

Such a form of poetry is always, consequently, unequal to itself, is radically self-contradicted. As image succeeds to image, the discourse accumulates a structure that grows increasingly overdetermined. Every part becomes open to invasion from every other part, nor are those 'parts' always what we think they are. The *Cantos* runs to many hundreds of pages, but it also runs to many decades of time; and histories which did not even exist when the first canto was produced come to impinge upon it later, and to force it to be seen, and read, in other terms and contexts.

The paranoia which some critics have noticed in the poem—the stylistic screed we saw in the Hell Cantos, the theme of the universal conspiracy of bankers and Jews—is a reflex of those contradictions. Such passages, particularly when they involve explicit presentations of Pound's anti-Semitism and fascism, come in for the heaviest kind of censure, or contempt, from most readers now. The following lines from Canto L, for example, are simply dismissed by John Lauber:

> And Ferdinando Habsburg . . .
> got back a state free of debt
> coffers empty
> but the state without debt

> England and Austria were for despots without commerce
> considered
>   put back the Pope but
> reset not republics: Venice, Genova, Lucca
> and split up Poland in their soul was usura
> and in their hand bloody oppression
> and that son of a dog, Rospigliosi,
> came into Tuscany to make serfs of old Tuscans.
> S . . t. on the throne of England, s . . t. on the Austrian sofa
> In their soul was usura and in their minds darkness
> and blankness, greased fat were four Georges
> Pus was in Spain, Wellington was a jew's pimp
> and lacked mind to know what he effected.
> 'Leave the Duke, Go for Gold!'
> In their souls was usura and in their hearts cowardice
> In their minds was stink and corruption
> Two sores ran together, Talleyrand stank with shanker
> and hell pissed up Metternich   (L. 248)

I have quoted somewhat more of the passage than Lauber because it is important to see what the lines are about in literal fact: that is, they develop a commentary on the restoration of the European thrones and dominions in the aftermath of the French Revolutionary and Napoleonic Wars.[31] One might add, in passing, that what Pounds says here is approximately what one will find in Byron's and Shelley's various commentaries on the European settlement engineered by England after the Napoleonic Wars.[32]

That said, one must observe as well that Lauber has not *read* the passage, he has simply reacted to—recoiled from—Pound's offensive rhetoric. Are we to think that a writer of Pound's skill was not *aware* of what he was doing, that he simply *missed* a shot at the beautiful here and lapsed into his anti-Semitic invective? Surely not, and when readers dismiss writing of this kind they are often merely exposing their own failures of intelligence—specfically, their failure to read, and to think through their reading.

Pound's anti-Semitism and fascism are important, in this context, because they can serve readers of the *Cantos* as convenient excuses

---

[31] For annotations see Terrell, *Companion*, i. 194–5. But Terrell believes Pound is only thinking of the Congress of Vienna (181) whereas he in fact has in mind the arrangements made there as well as the later rearrangements made at the Congress of Verona (182).

[32] See especially Byron's mordant late satire *The Age of Bronze* (1823).

not to read and not to think, and to believe that Pound—when he writes as an anti-Semite and a fascist—is unthinking as well. This is a great and a typical mistake among readers of the *Cantos*. The passage from Canto L, for example, uses its offensive rhetoric precisely as part of its strategy to challenge and call out the reader. If we lapse away by imagining (for example) that an absence of beauty here is a sign of bad writing, we shall merely have exposed our own habits of bad reading.

Beauty is not the issue here, any more than pleasure or beauty must be the criteria by which we measure the presence of poetry. Any careful reading of Rossetti, for instance, will reveal how a good writer may use the beautiful as an instrument of terror, or may expose the nightmare of pleasure and even happiness. Such writing is typical of the late nineteenth century, and of course Pound is a direct inheritor of that kind of writing.

Pound's writing is not devoted primarily to beauty, it is devoted to intelligence (and this frequently in its own despite). Beauty is one of the devices of intelligence in his work—and ugliness is another. Pound made this very clear very early, as we see in his essay 'The Serious Artist'. There he makes an important distinction between what he called 'the art of diagnosis and the art of cure' (45). The one he associated with 'ugliness' and the other with 'beauty', and he went on to observe: 'The cult of beauty and the delineation of ugliness are not in mutual opposition' so far as art is concerned. 'If the poets don't make certain horrors appear horrible who will?', Pound asked Felix Schelling. 'All values ultimately come from our judicial sentences. (This arrogance is not mine but Shelley's, and it is absolutely true. . . .)' (*L* 249).

Pound's writing has its failures, to be sure, but we should not be too quick in judging when and where these failures occur. Many of the *Cantos*'s self-contradictions, as we have seen, are anything but signs of weak writing. In the present instance, moreover, we confront a passage which fairly *announces* its call upon the intelligence of the reader. I am not thinking merely of the line 'and lacked mind to know what he effected'—with all that it must imply in context. Observe as well the beginning of the passage, and especially the fall of the word 'considered'. The spatial management of the text is excellent in that it directs our attention to the acts of mind with which 'England and Austria' were engaged in the immediate aftermath of the wars with Napoleon. The word also comes as a challenge to readers, to think in their turn about those events, to imagine *how* those events might be judged, and *why* anyone in 1937 might 'consider' such a re-consideration important.

From *our* point of view, here in 1988, we likewise have some thinking to do. If we attend to the style of the passage, for example, we will see how the whole movement pivots around the verse 'and split up Poland in their soul was usura'. This line releases a burst of energy by refusing to insert the stop after 'Poland' which the prose syntax calls for. The text refuses even a caesura and the consequence is an extraordinary leap in pace and tone.

So far as the sense of the passage is concerned, the line is equally crucial in that it centralizes 'Poland' as a figure of international political and economic manipulation. Pound is asking us to think back to the years 1817–22 and to the restoration of the European thrones under the leadership of England. The text recalls in particular the settlement of Poland, which involved, among other things, England's callous breach of the promises she had made to Polish patriots who were seeking freedom from Russian control. Tossing Poland to Russia was part of the European 'settlement', as were various other moves—Pound alludes to some of them—to ensure that hereditary and church power would be secured against the growing surge throughout Europe for nationalist autonomy.

The poetic effect here is all the more powerful because the lines are stylistically 'objectivist'. The deployment of this style, however, produced consequences for the poem that Pound—in trying to control his work—certainly did not foresee. First-person authority is a useful device for supplying poetry with an (illusory) resort from ideology, a stylistic 'place' which is imagined to be non-ideological. An objectivist procedure removes that particular resort, and the consequence is what has sometimes been called 'naked poetry', that is, a poetry whose illusion is that no part of the poetry will be set aside in a position of privilege—in this case, that no part of the poetry will be imagined as free of ideology.

Pound's satire on the crass politics of the restoration is one part of the ugliness in this passage, but the lines, once again, turn back on themselves and set off in pursuit of other forms of ugliness. 'Pus was in Spain, Wellington was a jew's pimp' is more than an incredibly clever (and incredibly offensive) satire on the suppression of the newly fledged Spanish patriotic revolution, more than an attack on the economic hegemony England was establishing for herself in

Europe. The style of the line is that of the Hell Cantos, and the phrase 'A jew's pimp'—in the context of the poem—establishes (and re-establishes) many connections besides the immediate one to Baron Rothschild.

'Jew's pimp' is not just 'anti-Semitic', it is anti-Semitic in a context of great complexity and concreteness. The phrase cannot be 'controlled' in the way that Pound, and Yeats, imagined that poetry could and should be controlled. As a consequence, the passage yields to its internal contradictions and over-determined pressures. The attack upon the European settlement does not here specifically mention Napoleon, though he is a major figure throughout Canto L (and elsewhere in the *Cantos*), where his energy is presented to contrast with his monarchical enemies: 'the Austrian sofa . . . greased fat [of the] four Georges'. But the *Cantos* cannot control the figure of Napoleon, any more than Napoleon—genius that he was—could control the world, or even his own destiny. There is a 'minds darkness' that goes beyond the darkness of monarchical wickedness or English political cynicism and that sweeps up Napoleon and all his related poetical *figurae*—Mussolini, Hitler, Sigismundo, Ezra Pound; and it is a darkness set in motion through the objectivism of Pound's work which, as the convict of its own illusions, is forced to place all its particular judgements before the bar of a supervening judgement. That supervening judgement is not a set of precepts or ideas, it is rather the law of this work's poetic style.[33]

The demon and the hero—the Jew (or Wellington) on one hand, and Napoleon on the other—are the text's ideological figures of ugliness and beauty, but their over-determined relations with other figures and texts in the *Cantos* cuts them loose from a fixed law and order. Consequently, what is horrible in these lines will appear as one thing to Pound while it will seem quite another to John Lauber, or to me, or—I dare say—to my readers. The lines make 'certain horrors appear horrible', and they do it in the way that poetry always does, by opening to critical thought those ideologies to which the poetry has commited itself.

And we must say 'ideologies', in the plural, because the commit-ments are as various as all those who will have ever been engaged with the poetry. Pound's objectivism collapses the distinction between

---

[33] See Kenner, *The Pound Era*, 444: 'Pound sought to outwit connoisseurship by devising a style inseparable from what it delivered'. And he succeeded, thereby creating a style which made his own poem subject to its own structures of judgement.

'writer' and 'reader'. We see this most clearly when we remember that Pound is writing this canto in the context of 1936–7. At that time the Polish Question once again was a crucial focus of European political interests; indeed, in 1936–7, if one took the Polish point of view, England's soul was indeed 'consumed with usura', and equally indifferent to Poland's political fate with respect to Russia and Germany. We forget that in the years immediately before the war England was anything but a friend to Poland, and that Poland regarded English policy with the deepest suspicion.

The general point, however, is that this text calls upon us to read with accuracy and intelligence, and in particular to consider the 'repeat in history' which it is imagining. Equally important to see, however, is that reading with intelligence does not necessarily entail agreeing (or disagreeing) with some or all or any of the judgements set forth in Pound's text. Those judgements, having been committed to the poem, have thereby submitted themselves to judgement in their turn.

In this way Pound's texts, like Byron's, enter a dialogue with their readers; this is what Pound, like Byron before him, wanted. Our text from Canto L calls out for reciprocal acts of thought from its readers. Such judgements often, as we have seen, work to expose the contradictions which the Poundian texts generate, and these antithetical readings are no more than what the poem expects from us.

But what of our failures to read, the lapses of intelligence to be discovered in those who look at Pound's poem? Does the work expect from its readers that seeing they may not see, and hearing they may not hear? In an important sense I think it does. Pound's texts make serious demands upon those who take them up, and the incredible arrogance of his work often functions, stylistically, as a cunning temptation to the reader's weakness. The poem has many resources for exposing critical thoughtlessness; one of its most effective may be located exactly in those passages where readers feel—out of their horror or out of their sympathy—that they have no difficulty in understanding. Here it is that Pound's work will commonly catch us at our worst, and expose us as that hypocritical reader known so well to Byron and to Baudelaire.

So we may say that the poem's processes overwhelm, and are overwhelmed by, its own judgements and illusions. The work reads itself in its own despite, and in doing so licenses our critical judgements of the work's fascism. But if we 'later' readers then imagine that the hells are here for 'other' people, for fascists and anti-Semites like Pound, we shall have fallen to the same illusion which led Pound initially to believe he could control and define the significance of his text's satire against England, against Jews, against usurocracy. Poems have hells and heavens for us, and those places are rarely what they seem to us to be.

When Pound was writing the Pisan Cantos, his gaolers became suspicious that he might be producing some kind of coded discourse, perhaps even fascist propaganda. To allay such apprehensions he sent a 'Note to [the] Base Censor' (the pun no doubt intended) in which he gave assurances that the new cantos 'contain nothing seditious', and 'nothing in the way of cypher or intended obscurity'.[34] Though he was telling the truth, it was only the truth as he knew it, and by no means the whole truth. If the new Cantos contained 'nothing seditious', they were still wedded to fascist ideology. But the commitment is plain to see and so the cantos were also, to that extent, not written in cipher.

None the less, the poem is (still) being written in a kind of encrypted discourse, because it is still sending messages, making communications, which Pound, the maker of the scripts, cannot master. These are not symbolic scripts, teasing and suggestive, but ideogrammatic ones: bold, expository, completely materialized. Blake would have said that Pound's work was being dictated from eternity in order that the truth, or the many genealogies of good and evil, might be revealed. The *Cantos* is remarkable because when we read it—the whole of it and not simply selected parts—we are prevented from lapsing into transcendental hermeneutics in either of its two predominant forms: the *voluptas* of a pure appreciation ('Gods float in the azure air'), or the *superbia* of final judgements ('malevolent stupidities and stupidities'). We are forestalled from these positions because the *Cantos* has been there, in each case, before us, and has displayed the consequences.

VI

Yeats's efforts to understand the *Cantos* were not, finally, successful. He misread the work because he wanted the *Cantos* to be something other than what it is. This misreading was first set out in the small

---

[34] C. David Heymann, *Ezra Pound: The Last Rower* (London, 1976), 172.

book we glanced at earlier, *A Packet for Ezra Pound*, where Yeats sent his younger friend an appropriate, if highly equivocal, gift. The 'packet' is in three parts: an opening section where Yeats makes a brief representation of the *Cantos* against the background of Pound's life at Rapallo; the central part—the gift proper—which is titled 'Introduction to the Great Wheel' and which contains a kind of synopsis of the growth and key features of *A Vision*; and finally a concluding (rather than a covering) letter 'To Ezra Pound'.

Yeats associates his own work on *A Vision* with the *Cantos* for very specific reasons. In the first place, he sees an analogy between this chaotic project of Pound's and the 'scattered sentences' (12) of his wife's automatic writing. Secondly, he judges that *A Vision* represents a triumph over the randomness of immediate experience and circumstance, and hence that it may provide Pound with a model, or norm, for a work like the *Cantos*, where Pound was being 'carried beyond reason'. Yeats gives Pound a glimpse of the Great Wheel, the totalized body of fate within which all reality may find its appropriate place.

The figure presiding over the Great Wheel, according to Yeats, is an image 'from Homer's age', a primitive form removed 'from Plato's Athens, from all that talk of the Good and the One, from all that cabinet of perfection' (35). The figure is Oedipus:

When it was already certain that Oedipus would bring himself under his own curse he still questioned, and when answered as the Sphinx had been answered, stricken with that horror which is in 'Gulliver' and in the 'Fleurs du Mal', he tore out his own eyes. . . . He knew nothing but his own mind, & yet because he spoke that mind fate possessed it and kingdoms changed according to his blessing & his cursing. . . . I think that he lacked compassion seeing that it must be compassion for himself.   (35–6)

Yeats deplored Pound's passion for politics and social reform—'all that cabinet of perfection'—and urged him, with this powerful imagining of Oedipus, to separate his art from his materials of art. The poet must represent, not be, Oedipus, just as the poem must rise above the horrors it takes up. But Pound was bent on exploring precisely those relations which Yeats, by a kind of categorical imperative, refused to consider. To imagine the poet as Oedipus—which is precisely what Pound did—was too cruel an imagination for Yeats. Better to imagine him as Homer, whose blindness is not linked to confusion but to a clarified and fufilling insight.

That is the poetic imagining which Pound too wanted, but in the event he reached a different conclusion. The passionate endurance of his quest for a 'totalitarian' form, and its rooted mistakenness, have their analogues in Yeats and in that figure of Oedipus. The *Cantos* expresses the pursuit of totality, as Yeats guessed, but it turns the screw on Yeats's representation. In Pound, only the work has 'Total Form', there is no primal vision or ultimate knowledge. As a consequence, the work is equal to itself in a sense that neither Pound nor Yeats had thought: every part of the work, productive and reproductive, stylistic and contextual—every synchronic aspect and every diachronic phase—impinges on every other. Coming in judgement, the work thereby sets in motion a series of second comings by which it finds itself made subject to continuous judgement.

The effect reminds me of the message, and in certain cases the medium, of many Pre-Raphaelite poems. Rossetti's work we have already examined in such a perspective, but I am thinking now of Swinburne's 'Hertha' and, perhaps even more, of that impressive conclusion to 'A Forsaken Garden':

> As a god self-slain on his own strange altar,
> Death lies dead.

In the *Cantos* Pound used the Blakean phrase 'furious from perception' to describe both himself and Adolf Hitler (Cantos XC and CIV). It was a phrase he meant to associate with a certain form of the 'minds darkness', a kind of error which he wanted his text to judge *as* error, but not as fundamental error. It was an error, in other words, that he was prepared to forgive (in himself and in others). 'But there is a blindness that comes from inside' (CIV. 741), the text adds, thereby gesturing towards a more fundamental error which will not be forgiven, a kind of sin against the light.

Pound meant to except Hitler and himself from an accusation of that sin, but the *Cantos* will not permit it. The blindness that comes from inside is no more exceptional than are those favoured and furious perceptions. Yeats's pitiless figure, hovering above the text, drains it of all its compassionate illusions. This is why the *Cantos* is not, finally, a tragic work.[35] It would be something far worse—something cruel, and utterly void of pity and compassion—were it not

---

[35] Pound's final remark in his interview with Donald Hall points toward the 'tragic' reading of the *Cantos*: 'Somebody said that I am the last American living the tragedy of Europe' (DH 51). This seems to me a sentimental, and finally a pathetic, observation coming from Pound.

simply something different, something which, like the lives we know, turns alternately through pity and indifference, evil and beauty. Submitting itself to those same contradictions, the work embodies a disturbing mode of truth: equivocal authority, uncertain knowledge— a fascist, and not a Daniel, come to judgement. For the documents of civilization—the writings of the great poets, the readings of the high-minded critics—are all of them, as Benjamin said, equally and at the same time documents of barbarism.

Towards a Literature of Knowledge

We are surrounded by emptiness, but it is an emptiness filled with signs.

HENRI LEFEBVRE, *Everyday Life in the Modern World*

The text will be as wonderful as the falling star of its original, the world.

BARRETT WATTEN, 'Conduit' XII

ANCIENT wisdom tells us that poets and prophets are in some way crippled, that a price has to be paid for the gift of imaginative vision. Even so urbane a poet as Horace thought this, and Shelley expressed an approximate idea in his more socially activist texts—in 'Julian and Maddalo', for example: 'Most wretched men| Are cradled into poetry by wrong,| They learn in suffering what they teach in song.'

This idea has generated a paradoxical, even a contradictory image of the poet in society. On the one hand poets can be seen as figures of privilege and reverence, the possessors of special insights and *conscience*. Homer and David are our models of such an imagination. On the other they may be regarded as relatively unimportant functionaries in the social body—amusing, perhaps even charming, but in the end ornamental figures useful to 'swell a progress, start a scene or two'. When Ulysses comes home to cleanse his house, he treats his court poet, his Homer, with the condescension of a man who understands the actual structure of social values and political power.

Wordsworth's thought that the poet is 'a man speaking to men' is important because it cut through the invidious distinctions on either hand of the conventional paradox. Hazlitt was one of the earliest people to understand the real significance of Wordsworth's 'levelling' idea. The Wordsworthian thought is not that poets are the spokesmen of worldly or transcendental powers; rather, they represent an ideal of communicative interchange—Wordsworth called it 'sympathy'—in which the power of authority and domination has been removed.

Later, Wordsworth and his reactionary interpreters Coleridge and De Quincey would do what they could to transform and undermine this original democratic breakthrough which had been made in the field of imagination. Hazlitt's subsequent critique of 'the literature of power', and of the privilege which such a literature gave to the ideas and the images—ultimately, to the illusions—of power, is an effort to recover and restore the original Wordsworthian insight.

Today we begin to unbuild the literature of power by a Blakean retreat and recovery, by unravelling that fatal thread of ideas running through the past two centuries to the effect that poetry gives us the best that has been known and thought in the world. Blake's idea was rather that poetry gives a body to falsehood, not a body to truth—that its truth-content lies precisely in its ability to reveal and set in operation 'the furnaces of Los[s]', where the body of error is created for its own self-destruction. The furnaces of Los are at once creators and destroyers.

This Blakean insight helps to explain the significance of writers like Byron, Rossetti, and Pound. None has been easily assimilated by the culture-industry until a careful screening process is set in motion, to civilize that in them which seems too nihilistic, too useless, too savage. After Blake, however, such writing approaches the truth of the world by turning literature against itself. What is important in this writing is what Adorno called 'the determinate negation of the status quo',[1] the refusal to sing the praises of 'the detestable Gods of Priam' and the men who set up such gods. The poets of Greece and the poets of Israel—Arnold's Hebrews and Hellenes—have alike pursued those gods, as Blake saw so very clearly, and their pursuit would be, as Blake said, 'a lasting witness against them'.[2] Pound was perhaps the last who would want to row in the terrible ships which sail toward glory along the cruel seas of power. His experience is therefore not merely an apocalypse of the literature of power, it is a prophecy of what must come, what has always come, to those who sell their souls to power.

We move toward a literature of knowledge when we understand that 'Truth is the antithesis of existing society.'[3] It is this insight which grounds the critical work, so different in other respects, of

---

[1] Theodor Adorno, *Aesthetic Theory* (London, 1984), 472.
[2] For the two Blake quotations see *Milton* 14: 15 and Blake's 'Annotations to . . . Watson' (p. 8).
[3] Adorno, *Aesthetic Theory*, 279.

Bataille, Benjamin, and Adorno. The premise leads Adorno, for example, to the following remarkable (Hegelian) observations:

> It is through elemental force that art becomes spiritual, not through the ideas it embodies. The elemental is intentionless and therefore receptive to spirit. The dialectic of spirit and the elemental is the truth content. . . . Kant's idea of art implicitly contained a notion of subservience or service. This view has to be refuted: art becomes human only when it gives notices that it will not play a serving role. The opposite ideology of art's service to humanity is incompatible with real humanity. It is art's inhumanity alone that bespeaks its faith in mankind.[4]

Observing the power of the consciousness-industries, Adorno sees that 'no art work escapes complicity with untruth, the untruth of the world' that appears (though it is not in fact) 'outside' the aesthetic domain.[5] That 'world outside' is the world of commodity exchange, Wordsworth's world of getting and spending and false utility. Poetry works in and through such a world and thence absorbs it within its own processes; its special privilege, however, is to render that world unconsumable, to re-present it as a set of dysfunctions and incommensurables.

This truth-content of poetical work is not simply a function of (Socratic) reflection, however, which is what Adorno, and even Bataille, often suggest. Poetry's negative or critical awareness emerges because it has embraced 'knowledge' in the modern scientific sense of that term. That is to say, poems have factive dimensions which it is essential to 'know' before one can begin to approach their truth-contents.

Poems are, first of all, acts of representation; as such, they can only be read when the entire facticity of those acts is raised into consciousness. The acts of poetry are begun and carried forward in specific socio-historical circumstances, and the poetical investments in those circumstances—what poems give and receive back—are not merely recorded in the poems, they are executed in them. Scholarly archives are far more than just convenient devices for making scholastic forays into the literary past; they embody that field of mutual presences and interpenetrations which we designate as the socio-history of poetical work. Fascism, Lady Byron, and the reviews of Rossetti's *Poems* (1870) are part of the knowledge developed through the work of Pound, Byron, and Rossetti; they are not

---

[4] Ibid. 281.   [5] Ibid. 475.

extraneous facticities, irrelevant to the poetry. They are essential poetic materials. We gain our knowledge of them, our poetical knowledge of them, through our literary archives. When Keats distinguished the 'poet' from the 'dreamer' in 'The Fall of Hyperion', he made a comment about the archival, the factive, dimension of art.

Equally essential, and factive, is the historicity of such materials, that is, the ways in which they have been implicated in the poetry over time: the degrees to which they have been read or unread in the poems, the vantages from which they have been read, the emphases they have been given. The interpretation of poems is not a revelation of meaning but a history thereof, a 'matter of facts' (though not only a matter of facts). These determinate matters are as much a part of poetry's evolving bodies of falsehood as the most originary materials associated with the writing.

The remarkable feature of poetical work lies in its power to license many different organizations of these materials, many conflicting and incommensurable organizations. These too are matters of fact, though the scale of their facticity is larger than the scale of many other matters of fact (e.g. those that appear to us through our glosses on particular words or passages). In the end poems emerge, at the experiential level, as those 'pictures of great detail' which so fascinated an historicist scholar like Milman Parry.

Situated at such an experiential level, poetry aspires towards the condition of knowledge. Julia Kristeva was keenly aware of this artistic threshold (it is at once an opportunity and a limitation) when she distinguished poetry's moment of 'experience' from its moment of 'practice'.[6] Through poetry one comes to see how 'experience outruns conception', but that breakthrough in understanding is only a preliminary cognitive moment, and cannot by itself deliver poetry from reactionary hands. If experience outruns conception, however, it does not outrun 'practice'; for the latter is 'experience' operating in its most complete form, as a set of determinate, and more or less deformed, aspirations and desires.

We glimpse this even in the most passivist and abstract manifestos of the imagination—for example, in the conclusion to Tennyson's 'Ulysses':

> For all experience is an arch wherethrough
> Gleams that untravelled world whose margin fades
> For ever and for ever as I move.

[6] See her *Revolution in Poetic Language* (New York, 1984), esp. Part IV.

Ulysses' movement is the sign of his desire, the praxis of his experienced knowledge of his world's untruth. Reading Tennyson's poem, we re-experience the conflict of that frustrated desire. The conflict is most starkly figured as the differential between Ulysses and his son Telemachus. That differential, however, is itself a conflicted sign, for we cannot attach unequivocal values (either positive or negative) to the 'work' chosen by either figure. Read in socio-historical terms, Telemachus is an image of Victorian middle-class responsibility, Ulysses of Victorian imperialist energy; and both are, therefore, broken and corrupted forms of praxis. Furthermore, the total structure of Tennyson's poem replicates the 'untruth' which its images display. Placing its words in the mouth of Ulysses, the poem is as immobilized in untruth as are the figures of its narrative.

In such circumstances one is 'lost on both sides', and Tennyson's work remains completely true to that condition of loss. It is a poem about the desire to imagine and execute moral choices, and about the inability to do so. Yet as a work of desire the poem supervenes its own immobilization. Here untruth is so perfectly executed that it generates the wild and incoherent desire of a truth which has passed through the arch of experience into the world of practice:

> To strive, to seek, to find, and not to yield.

This final image defines a movement that will not 'yield' to what it has sought after and finally found. It is the figure of a true desire, the *eros* of a body of falsehood, of a world of untruth. It is the poem's answer to the conflicted structure in which, and to which, it was born.

The cognitive dynamic played out through poetic discourse is not confined, however, to the closed circle of Hegelian, or Socratic, reflection. The dynamic involves real, objective knowledge because the poetic field remains, finally, under the dominion of experience and not of consciousness. We acknowledge that experiential dominion when we make our factive explorations through the literary archive—a depository which, like the Nature of the scientist, draws our desire and exhausts our cognition. Poetry and the meanings of poetry are never equal to themselves, even conceptually, because their histories are open-ended in all three phases of their temporalities—in their futures, obviously, but in their pasts and their presents as well. We move toward a literature of knowledge along the trajectory of a desire to change what we believe to be wrong, to repair what we see is broken, and to redeem what we know has been lost. Through poetry we learn how we cannot succeed in any of these quests, and how, on that very account, we are called upon to maintain them, and 'not to yield' to their repeated, illusory achievement.

Index